T0146738

America Calls to Me

The Story of a Refugee Boy's Journey

Martin Toe

WESTBOW
P R E S S®
A DIVISION OF THOMAS NELSON
& ZONDERVAN

WestBow Press books may be ordered through booksellers or by contacting:

WestBow Press
A Division of Thomas Nelson & Zondervan
1663 Liberty Drive
Bloomington, IN 47403
www.westbowpress.com
1 (866) 928-1240

ISBN: 978-1-5127-9347-5 (sc)
ISBN: 978-1-5127-9348-2 (e)

Library of Congress Control Number: 2017910046

Print information available on the last page.

WestBow Press rev. date: 6/26/2017

DEDICATION

Embrace gratitude, expressing thanks for all you have is
a lost emotion in our society.

Gene Connolly- Principal of Concord High School

ACKNOWLEDGMENTS

To my mother, Linda Tarwo and my dad Augustine Toe for loving me and for teaching me to be the man that I am today, to Sophie my sister, to Vivian my niece, to Geoffrey my brother, and to every man and woman who has helped us along the way.

Chapter 1

My name is Martin Toe. I was born in a province in the western part of Ivory Coast in a small town called La Sati, which is a few hours' travel away from the Cavalla River along the border with Liberia. While I was still a toddler, my mother and father relocated to a nearby town called Grabo. It was a great city, packed with diverse people from all around Africa and well known for its rough roads and commercial buses. The house that we lived in was made of bricks and mortar, with concrete floors that kept the house cool. The galvanized rooftop prevented the blazing heat from permeating our home during the dry season.

In 1999, I was three years old and the second youngest child of a well-respected and wealthy entrepreneur by the name of Linda Tarwo. I was a small, chubby kid with dark brown eyes, curly, black hair, and a big smile that captivated my mother's heart. I carried myself confidently throughout my adolescence. I knew I was wealthy and didn't have to worry about anything. I was always well fed and had plenty of entertainment to keep me preoccupied for as long as I wanted.

When you arrive at the bus station in my town, you'll notice the rigid walkways that once were paved. Along the side of the road, there are local stores, restaurants, and coffee shops. As you head on your way in and out of the small alleys, you will arrive at a marketplace several streets down from the barracks. Merchants, contractors, businessmen, and businesswomen gather here from all around the world to sell their products and services.

My mother understood the significance of being exposed to different areas and aspects of life. So, when my sister and I were old enough, she sent us to Grand-Béréby, near San-Pédro, in order for us to learn the culture and traditions of the people living in other areas of Ivory Coast. Our travels brought us to Abidjan—the capital of Ivory Coast—as well as the surrounding cities. We lived with my mother's close friend, Neheih Gaston.

My mother—like any mother—desired to give us the best opportunities. She didn't want us to think that the small town of Grabo was all there was to see in the world. There were different types of people who lived in Grabo. Not everyone was to be admired. Some were lazy and others worked hard. Some were deceitful, while others were honest. Some were hateful, and others were racist. However, there were those who were both compassionate and caring. Those people were only a handful of the personalities I was exposed to while I lived in Grabo.

People knew who I was because of my mother. In my young mind, I didn't understand the significance of politics. I was oblivious as to why people bickered over trivial matters. Most of the adults who lived in town lived quiet and peaceful lives by avoiding conflict. Growing up, I didn't know if I wanted to be a football player, a businessman like my mother, or a doctor. I just knew, one day, I was going to be an adult like everyone else. When I would go to the marketplace, people would say, "That is Linda's child." It felt good to be recognized in town by the locals; but, at the same time, there was a lot of pressure on me to behave in a respectful manner.

Unluckily, I was not the sharpest tool in the box—at least by most people's standards. Because of my socioeconomic status, I was usually picked on and shunned by other kids. On top of being bullied by the others, I just wasn't a smart kid or the most liked. The teacher would consistently whip my butt every time I got an answer wrong in class. Often, I would skip class with the other kids because I didn't feel like I belonged.

One day, my mom came home early from one of her business trips. "What are you doing here?" she asked, hoping to hear a logical response. "Aren't you supposed to be in school?"

"The teacher was going to beat me," I accused. My brain scrambled to invent a story. "So I thought I'd come home before he got to me."

"That is not a good excuse to not be in school right now, Martin."

I stared at the concrete floor. "Yeah, I know, I just didn't want to get beaten today. I'll go back tomorrow …," I mumbled as my voice drifted off.

Tuma was listening. She made her way from the kitchen after Mom was done talking to me. "Martin," she said with hate clear in her voice and posture. "If I was still your age and I had the chance to go to school, I would do something to become someone great. Don't waste your chance." I nodded my head in agreement with her, knowing full well I was afraid of going back to the school—especially after I had lost the book my professor had lent me. At a young age, Tuma's mother had passed away; since then, the trauma has plagued her. Tuma's mother and Mom were sisters, and because of the relationship, Mom ended up taking Tuma in and treating her as her own daughter. Tuma even called her "my other mom."

My father left my mother, my sister, and me to go back to Liberia to find new opportunities. He was a tall, handsome, black man with curly hair that glistened with silver and gray. His dark brown eyes were filled with wonder and laughter. He was a brilliant man, both well-educated and well-recognized.

After settling in Liberia, he decided to come back to Grabo to persuade us to go with him. He spent the whole day trying to persuade us. At first, it sounded like a dream come true. For the longest time, we hadn't heard from Dad. Tuma used to tell me he didn't care for us, and I believed it. Dad always had his way, but not this time. This time, things were not the same as they used to be. The history between my mother and my father was bittersweet. There was a time when Dad just couldn't be refused, but this time, his proposition was not well received. My mother declined his request. Before he made his journey back to Liberia, my father gave presents to Sophie and me and promised once again to come back to get us. After a time of not seeing him, my heart grew bitter, and the hope of us reuniting slowly faded away. I went back to the life that I knew—the comfort of the everyday things to which I was accustomed. I reminded myself that life would always be enjoyable with my mother.

Chapter 2

Whenever I close my eyes, I still can revive the memories of my old home just as it was. I can imagine the trees in my backyard swaying back and forth as the early summer breeze slips through the crack of my window. Children are running through the streets flying their kites, and my mother is coming home from work and being happily greeted by my sister Sophie and me. The sweet aroma of palm butter billows into the air from Tuma's cooking, and the other two girls are helping to clean the house while making time to shower and prepare to eat. I'd always tried to avoid doing chores by going out and playing a pickup game of soccer, I would be back just in time to eat.

Tuma or one of the other girls would tell us a good story that had some type of moral or valuable lesson. The house we lived in had three bedrooms, one living room, and one built-in bathroom. I had to share a room with one of the older girls my mom had adopted because at that time, I feared sleeping alone in a room by myself. I would keep my valuable possessions in a box that had a lock on it that only I could open. On my bed was the blanket that the adopted girls' mother had given to me as a gift. In Sāto, girls did not get an education; they were required to stay home, cook, clean, and one day, have an arranged marriage. The girls' mother let my mom adopt them so that they could get an education and have the best opportunities in life. The girls' parents couldn't afford to send them to school, so this was the only way to do so. Each night before going to sleep, Mom would say to me, "Good night." I would always have a million question to ask before finally falling asleep.

While my sister and I were young, my mother told us stories about the Liberian civil war that had brought her, my father, and countless other Liberians to Ivory Coast. Mom and Dad are from the River Gee county of Liberia. My mother came from the tribe of Glaro people, and her father passed away while she was still a young woman. She did what she could to get a good education for herself. When school was over, she would cut wood and sell it at the marketplace to pay for her books and tuition fees. She was bright and outgoing; there was nothing that she couldn't do. People loved her in her community, and her peers respected her.

The First Liberian Civil War of 1989 lasted through 1997. The fall of Samuel Doe's regime led to the killing of over 600,000 people. My mother and my father were lucky to flee the country along with others. After crossing the Cavalla River together, they traveled into Ivory Coast together in hopes of escaping the chaos and in search of a new start in Ivory Coast. The one thing that I learned about history is that if you don't learn from it, you are bound to repeat it.

Chapter 3

January 1, 2000 New Year was my favorite holiday, especially in Grabo; it was well celebrated by almost everyone in different customs and traditions. People of Grabo prepare for this holiday at least one month in advance. It would begin by buying presents, making costumes and decorating their houses. One of the traditions of the town was, on New Year's Day, all the kids would dress up in their best clothing and go door-to-door. When the party opened the door, the kids would say "bonne année" (Happy New Year). The party would then answer back "bonne a fêté" (good celebration). The party would then offer the children something of value. My favorite part of the holiday was getting money. Depending on how good your costume was and the doors you went to, you could end the day pocketing at least a couple hundred dollars.

On New Year's Day, my brother JJ and I would go knocking door-to-door saying, "bonne année." I would be dressed up as a businessman in the three-piece suit minus the suitcase. Clean cut, with a pair of black shoes to match the attire. I could tell JJ was trying hard not to be jealous. He had just come back to visit us. Instead of living with us, he stayed with his step grandma. JJ and I had different dads but that never affected our relationship. He put on his best clothes, turned towards me and asked, "What do you think?"

"It looks great!" I answered smiling.

"You think so?" he asked, hoping to provoke a more positive reaction.

"Yeah," I replied, scrambling my brain to find something nice to say. "If I wasn't wearing this thing, I'd wear your clothes."

He grinned at me and said, "Okay then, let's switch!" He reached over and started forcefully removing my suit off of me.

"No, you're too big for it," I cried out, hoping he'd relinquish his grip.

"You're right," he responded while losing his grip, "that's what you get for running your big mouth."

I blinked back the tears threatening to fall from my eyes and didn't dare tell Mom about the whole situation. Whenever JJ came around, it was never an extended stay. As soon as he got what his grandmother sent him to get, he would return home. I never understood why I used to think that he hated us and was envious of my sister and me, but that wasn't the case. He was a happy kid who just enjoyed spending time with his grandparents and taking care of them.

As he leaned on the doorpost and watched bypassers go by, he asked, "Are you ready?"

"Yeah, I'm ready," I responded back, wiping the tears from my eyes.

On our way, we saw a girl from my neighborhood playing in her yard. "Who is that?" he asked.

Trying to impress him I said, "That girl? She's my girlfriend."

He couldn't believe his ears. "No, she's not," he whispered. "I'm going to ask her."

"Go ahead, do it," I said confidently, not thinking he would ask a stranger.

"Excuse me!" he yelled across the street. "My little brother told me you are his girlfriend?"

"I did not say that!" I yelled pounding my foot against the ground.

Overpowering my voice, he asked her "Is that right?"

"No, it's not true," she replied with a look of disgust.

I felt so embarrassed, and I knew from that day on, she and I could never be friends again. That was the last time I ever saw her. During the festivity, JJ poked jokes at me and told me that I was a bad liar. I hated being called a liar; this is an example of the small things big brothers did to get on your nerves. He knew how to push my buttons.

After stopping at a few wealthy people's houses, we had a few hundred dollars in our pockets. We covered about a good portion of the town. "Martin, let me hold the money so that you won't lose it." Being gullible, I handed it over to him, which was one of the worst decisions I'd made that day apart from telling him Doedoe was my girlfriend. "Let's go to the mechanics, they always have money," I requested.

"Yeah you're right, let's go," he said while stepping aside to let me lead.

When we got there the smell of car residue filled the air, and it was business as usual. I recognized a blue truck that belong to one of the businessmen that was a tenant in one of my Mom's houses. I figured we must be in the right place at the right time. Everyone seemed preoccupied with something; one man was working on the blue truck while another was sorting out paperwork. On top of that, the radio was blaring with a voice of a news reporter man speaking in a resounding thick French accent. We stood there awkwardly and watched the mechanics work.

"Martin,' JJ lowered his voice. "Aren't you going to say something to them?"

"Yeah give me a second," I said in a commanding tone, thinking of a way to approach the mechanics.

"We don't have all day you know," JJ said sternly.

I swallowed the spit in my mouth and started walking towards the mechanic working on the car.

JJ leaned over and whispered in my ear. "Tell him we want money."

"No," I said, quickly responding back. "That's not respectful."

"Sir, we came here to say bonne année," I blurted, surprising the mechanic who was working on the truck.

"Bonne année?" he asked quickly. "You do not know that la Guerre is coming?"

I looked over to JJ who was already making his way towards me. JJ leaned over to whisper. "I don't think he wants to give us money."

What does he mean by "la guerre?" I whispered back.

"I think it means war," JJ asserted back to me.

So I asked the mechanic "Who said that la guerre is coming?"

"It's all over the news," the mechanic warned, "go and tell your parents."

My brother and I quickly started making our way back home. On our way, we stopped at more houses hoping to make a few more dollars before getting home. One of the doors we knocked on belonged to a tall lady. When she opened the door, she asked, "Can I help you?"

"Bonne année!" I said out loud hoping to make her smile and hopefully securing a few bucks from her.

"No child, you need to go home right now and warn your family. Rebels are on their way."

I felt my heart sink into my stomach. "Okay!" I exclaimed.

Off we went racing back home to deliver the news to our mother. JJ had trouble breathing so whenever I was far ahead I would slow down for him to catch up. When we got home, I ran straight to my mother's room trying not to make a commotion. "Mom, Mom they said war is coming."

She quickly woke up from laying down and sat on the bed.

"Who said that?'

"The man on the radio."

Mom swiftly grabbed her flip flops, tied on her lapa skirt around her waist and hurried over to one of the condos occupied by a man named Soloe. A block away from where we lived, stood seven condos purchased and renovated by Mom and rented to tenants who were businessmen.

Soloe was a guy who liked listening to the news but didn't like to talk about politics. "Did you hear the news?" Mom asked Soloe as soon as he opened the door.

"What news?" one of the other young men who worked for Soloe responded.

"They say that rebels are heading this way," Mom said, hoping to find some answers.

"Oh, let's turn on the radio to see if it's true," Soloe suggested.

Soloe turned on his brand new radio. The radio was already stationed on the news, so everybody gathered around. JJ told the others what was going on as we listened. Our voices quieted to a stop, everyone listening intently to the news reporter with the thick French accent. I couldn't quite catch everything he was saying, but by the look on my mother's face, I could tell something was wrong.

Chapter 4

A few minutes later, Soloe turned the volume down and the adults started talking. In our culture, it was a show of respect that kids go elsewhere when the adults have a sensitive conversation. JJ, Sophie, the two adopted girls and I made our way back home, talking amongst ourselves. Tuma stayed behind and soon after made her way back home. Mom stayed behind and continued talking with Soloe and the other fellows.

For the first time in my life, I felt like the serenity I once knew was being threatened. Arriving at the house, Mom started talking to Tuma. Tuma didn't seem quite pleased to hear the news. She went to her room and started packing her things. Afterwards, my mother called to me and handed me some money, sending me out to the marketplace to get food. She explained: "Buy all the achecīr the woman is selling and buy twelve packs of sardines. If anyone asks you, tell them it's for my Mom."

"Okay," I replied and quickly raced into town. Achecīr is made from processed cassava fixed with plantains and fried fish. At my arrival the lady was packing up. I told her, "I want all the achecīr you have."

"Why?" she asked.

"It's for my Mom," I said.

I then picked up the twelve cans of sardines and raced back home. The house that was once filled with laughter was now filled with silence. I could see the girls were putting their things together. My sister Sophie was still with the girls and JJ was out of sight. My mother was in her room packing.

"Mom!" I called out.

"Martin, what is it?"

"I got the achecīr what do you want me to do now?" I asked, waiting for my next instruction.

"Go tell JJ to pack his stuff. We are leaving to Fetia tonight."

"Where is Feita and how far is it?" I asked her.

"It's past Sāto, 4 hours away from here!"

"When will we be back?" I asked, hoping to have a good estimate.

"It all depends on how fast this goes away."

Deep down I wanted it to last for a few weeks, so I didn't have to worry about going back to school. At the same time, I didn't want to leave the comfort that I was so familiar with. I feared to leave my friends behind and my potential girlfriend who apparently didn't know I liked her.

I found JJ sitting alone in the storage room staring into the distance. I stood and watched him, thinking to myself, '*what a strange kid*'. "JJ, are you alright?"

"I want to go back home," he answered with tears falling from his eyes.

"You can go back home after all this is over; it's not safe to go back home now."

"Who's going to take care of grandma? She has no one else."

"Don't worry, grandma can take care of herself; she's been taking care of herself every time she sends you here. Plus, we never get to see you that much. After all, when this is over Mom will send you back to grandma with lots of money."

He looked at me and smiled. "You think so?"

"Yes."

JJ was a caring soul, always willing to set aside his own agendas to do what's right. He was the second oldest brother, a natural leader and an optimist at heart. He got up, and we started packing our luggage. I was terrified and afraid of this moment, afraid of what lied ahead. I was scared of not knowing what life would be like if things didn't get better. I was afraid my family might split up or worse, someone getting hurt. I wanted to tell JJ that, but I didn't have it in me to do so. I could see that he wanted nothing more but to be with his grandma and he didn't know when he would see her again. Only time would tell.

Chapter 5

It had been almost seven months since I last stepped my foot out of town. I wasn't prepared or in shape for a long journey on foot. The streets were empty as far as the eye could see, silence filled the whole town. The once-decorated town now resembled a ghost town filled with closed doors and cracked opened windows.

Everybody was inside trying to figure out what they were going to do next. I could see families arguing in their houses through my window. Not long afterward, we saw the first family with their luggage on their head, heading toward Fetia.

It was a cheerless New Year's Day, as all the shops in town were closing. It was a sight of hopelessness and despair. If this was the beginning war pains, then I didn't want to know what war felt like. I decided to go outside one last time. I wanted to feel the cool breeze that always made me feel at home. Except this time, it just didn't feel right. I went back inside and everyone had packed and was ready to go. Tuma came up to me, hugged me and asked, "Are you ready?"

I looked at her and nodded my head, knowing that I still had a few more things to pack. I ran into my room and slipped a few t-shirts and pants into my backpack to take with me for the journey. Mom was ready; she had made her runs and had the house in order. She left one of the tenants to watch over the houses while we were gone and maintain the property if it was possible. My mother called us all together. The two girls who stayed with us; Kadisha and Brakisa, my deceased aunt's daughter Tuma, my sister Sophie, JJ and I held hands and prayed not knowing this would be our last prayer in this town together.

Instead of going into town and taking a bus like Mom usually does when going on her business trips, we took the back road that passed through the forest- a twenty-minute walk. As we came closer to the main road that led to the town of Fetia, a group of young men holding machetes barricaded the main road. Luckily for us, the back road was after their barricade. We exchanged greetings with them and kept on going. One of the fellows was speaking under his breath to the guy beside him about us, but we kept on walking as if nothing was wrong.

There was a forest on both sides of the road. I was in awe of the size and the majesty of the trees and the orchestra of birdsong with every step we took. I heard a monkey laughing. The evening sun began to rest down upon the trees, allowing the night sky to shine with silver stars. The night was upon us. A sign that said Sāto in crooked letters was written on a billboard. I was familiar with this town as Mom usually came here for business

18

trips and the people in this city loved her. Every time I came with her, a host family would welcome us into their home. They would prepare their traditional dish of bread and tea, which I didn't enjoy. After a good laugh, the mother and father of the family would then ask Mom if she would be interested in adopting one of their girls and raising them up in the city. Mom with her big heart would always try to find a way to make it work out.

Arriving in Sāto, we were happily welcomed by the family of the girls who stayed with us. Some of the kids from this town were fortunate to go to school, so I knew some of them from back home. They called kids like me who went to school in town "les enfants de la Ville" (city children). I asked Mom if I could go and play with the other kids.

I felt crushed when she said, "No. We are going to be leaving soon, early tomorrow morning, so you need to make sure you're well rested."

That night, I heard loud music coming from outside. Mom had told me not to leave the guest room, but the cheering, the noise, and the music was tempting. I poked my head outside and saw a girl walking by. I tried getting her attention by calling out to her.

"Hey, do you know what's going on?"

"It's the New Year celebration," she answered back as she made her way towards the music.

I quickly hopped out of bed. I put on some clothes, laced up my shoes and headed out the door towards the direction the music was coming from. Upon arriving, I saw a lot of kids in my age group. Some were much older, all dancing and celebrating the New Year. Two men were playing large xylophones and two other men played drums. They danced and yelled all night until they couldn't dance anymore. As the crowd faded, my eyes grew heavy, and I felt like it was time to go back to the guest room.

The next morning, I heard people talking outside. It was some young girls pumping water. I looked out my window and said hello them. They could tell that I wasn't from their town. They looked at me and giggled. I sat back on my bed, looking across the room at my suitcase. I put my stuff together, grabbed my toothbrush and toothpaste. I needed to fill my cup with water. I was curious, and I wanted to see where they were getting the water from. I followed the trail of water that was falling out of their water pots. I arrived at a place encompassed by four walls and a tall metal door coated in crimson. The chief of the town had the key to the door. He explained to me earlier that the gatekeeper would only open the door in the morning and during the evening. I asked a man standing at the door if I could get some water to brush my teeth. He nodded his head and let me enter. A bunch of girls were waiting in line for their turn to pump water. The girl in the front of the line saw I had a toothbrush in my hand and a cup. She signaled me to come up, so I quickly made my way up the stairs. I then asked her if it was okay if I pumped my own water. She nodded her head, and I made my way to the pump. I enjoyed the process of pumping the water, so I asked each girl next in line if I could pump the water for her. Before I knew it, I was all wet, and the guy at the door motioned for me to come down. He handed me my toothbrush and cup of water, and I said thanks before heading out. I went back to the guest room and changed into some dry clothes. I put the wet clothes into a plastic bag and shoved it into my bag. I gathered my stuff together and made my way back to the rendezvous point.

When I went to the spot, JJ was already sitting there next to Sophie's, Tuma and Mom's luggage. He was peering into the distance as if he was caught in between two different worlds.

"JJ," I murmured in a soft voice. He didn't answer so I said his name again, making sure to say it louder this time.

"Uh," he responded, snapping out of it.

"Are you okay?" I investigated, looking at him curiously.

"Don't be scaring people like that," he said angrily.

"Sorry man, just wanted to make sure you were okay."

"I'm fine."

"Where is Mom, Sophie and Tuma?" I demanded.

"Sophie and Tuma went to the bathroom," he answered, trying to avoid eye contact with me. After their bathroom break, Sophie and Tuma came back, and I about their night. I told them the story about last night's town celebration and asked them not to tell Mom. I knew Tuma was going to tell her, so I threatened to tell Mom her secrets if she dared.

The other two girls started walking towards where Tuma, JJ, Sophie and I were sitting. The older girl,

Kadisha, who shared the same room with me, hugged Tuma and Brakisa, the younger girl stood behind her shyly. After Tuma, she hugged Sophie, and then JJ. As she approached me, I asked her, "Are you guys coming with us?"

"We decided to stay with our parents," she responded, smiling back at me and the others.

I felt my heart shatter. As much as we had bonded with the girls and they had become family, I knew they also had a family that loved them and wanted them too. They talked with us for a few more minutes, wished us good luck then walked away. My mother made her way back from talking with the girls' family and giving them a gift of appreciation. As soon as she came, I asked her, "Can we go?"

"Yes, we will. Are you okay?" She asked, trying to figure out why I was eager to leave.

Tuma quickly interjected, "He's just mad the girls won't be joining us."

"Don't worry. After all this, they will come back."

That cheered me up. I felt hope spring up in me. We grabbed our luggage and once again we began to walk. Next stop would be Feita, a dreadful four-hour walk.

Hours passed as my family members listened to my moans and complaints. A hand shoved me from behind and I stumbled forward, almost falling on my face.

"Shut up you wimp." I turned my head to see who had pushed me. JJ, carrying his bag on his head, he saw the tears threatening to fall from my eyes. I tried to hold it back, but I couldn't. Every time I cried Mom would intervene, so he did the only thing that would stop my crying. "Do you want me to carry your bag?" he asked.

Wiping away the tears, I nodded my head. After carrying my bag for a long time, he handed it back to me. He repeated this a few times, and every time he asked I would sheepishly hand him back my bag.

The sun was beating on us, and sweat covered our faces only an hour ago, the heat wave of twelve o'clock upon us. We walked on the tinder forest road, regretting leaving our cozy home. We saw some people going in the opposite direction from where we were heading. Mom asked the group, "Where are you heading to."

"We are heading back from Sāto," claimed a lady carrying a basket on her head with a baby on her back tied in a lapa shirt.

"You're not too far away," the man trailing behind the woman interjected.

"Thank you. Safe journey," Mom answered back excitingly.

"Safe journey to you," implored the lady.

We trudged the last few miles beneath the relenting sun. Along the way, I daydreamed of being back home and lying on my bed, sleeping until all the pain felt underneath my feet from walking all day was gone. I imagined going to the market place and seeing all the merchants, the businessman, the stores and restaurants all opened filled with customers. I imagined eating achecīr with fried plantains and fried fish. I was hungry, and there was no food. I was thirsty, and there was no water to drink.

"We made it," said Tuma, while smiling excitedly into the distance "We've done it."

In the near distance was a small town of Fetia, resting near the banks of the Cavalla River, which separates the border of Ivory Coast and Liberia.

Chapter 6

Fetia was a beautiful panorama scene of nature and backyard gardens. The people in this town lived between the natural and artificial. They lived off the land, they were farmers, hunters, and gatherers. When we arrived in town, my Mom told us to wait by the junction. We watched her as she disappeared between the mud buildings and went off to go meet a friend. After a while, she came back. "We will be spending the night here," she said while picking up her bag.

"Outside?" I petitioned jokingly.

JJ chuckled.

"No," Mom answered back while leading the parade. "We will be spending the night at one of my friend's house, and tomorrow we will cross when things are situated."

We walked past an old man selling dry fish on the side of the road. He wasn't like the other vendors back home; he didn't try to get our attention or bargain with us to buy his fish. I stared at him, hoping for some eye contact, but he just stared straight ahead, not once looking up. "Stop looking at the old man," JJ chastised me while trying not to make eye contact with him.

I turned to face forward, but I was tempted to get one last look at him. We followed Mom on a small pathway pass some houses and gardens. I noticed that some of what they planted were ready to be harvested. The people of that town grew potatoes, beans, cucumbers, peppers, and tomatoes. We came to a tall house with one door and two small windows that let in sunlight. It was a two-room house, with a kitchen attached to the outside. There was a yard and behind it, like most of the houses, was a garden.

"We are going to be sleeping in their living room," Mom said after arriving at the door with a man standing there as if he had been waiting.

"No, not in this house. The boys will sleep in the living room. You and the girls share the room with my wife," said the owner of the house. For the first time in my life, I wanted to be a girl just so I could sleep in a comfortable room, where I'd be safe from little pests like mosquitoes.

The man's wife prepared a meal. My Mom offered to share the achecīr we were carrying. The owner of the household refused her offer and told her to keep it because we would need it for the journey. His wife served JJ and I. We ate from the same bowl while Sophie, Mom, Tuma, the wife, and her young daughter ate from another bowl. We ate until our stomachs were full. That night; Tuma didn't tell us a story, she told us to get ready for bed at an earlier time than usual.

I overheard the adults talking about people getting

sent back from the border. I feared having to walk back after coming so far. At the same time, I wanted life to go back to normal. JJ knew I was listening to the conversation as he was. He rolled over the mattress we were laying on to face me.

"I think we might be going back home tomorrow," he whispered.

"Do you really think so?" I questioned.

"Yeah, I just heard Mom and the guy saying no one is crossing the border."

"You're right," I answered back to him, "goodnight JJ."

"Goodnight."

I closed my eyes and tried to imagine home. I tried to picture the tree in my backyard, the cool breeze swaying the trees back and forth. Except for this time, something was wrong, the pictures that I could see so vividly was distorted. My mind was in turmoil, affecting my ability to focus on visualizing the home I left behind. I opened my eyes hoping to stay awake through the night, but my heavy eyelids closed shut and off to sleep I went.

The next morning everyone was up early. They were having breakfast; the girls were eating together and the owner of the house ate with JJ. I still felt sleepy as I walked over to Mom. She was also eating as I rested my head on her shoulders.

"MacMartin," she said calling me by the nickname she had given me at birth.

The owner smiled and said, "Oh don't worry little man, we have some food in that little bowl for you." He pointed at the only bowl on the table not being eaten from.

I was relieved from the thought that they had forgotten all about me and wanted to fill their stomachs. I asked the owner for water to wash my face and to brush my teeth, he pointed towards the corner where the girls were eating. After brushing my teeth, I grabbed the small bowl of rice and soup that was set aside for me and started eating. By that time everyone, else was already done eating. I took my time and savored every bite as if it was my last.

Mom and the owner of the house started talking about crossing once again. I wondered to myself if perhaps JJ was right, this was as far as the journey went. JJ and I didn't know what was going on, not even Tuma. I pestered JJ, trying to see if he had heard anything from Mom and the owner of the house.

"So what do you think?" I bid him, hoping to get some type of answer.

"I don't know, I haven't heard anything," he responded back.

I walked away and went to lay on the mattress that we had brought with us. We were able to bring it with us by folding and tying it so that someone in the group can carry it on his or her head. I thought about how long the journey would be if we decided to continue forward. I thought about how long it would be till we return back to our hometown. My thoughts carried my consciousness away until my eyes got heavy and I fell asleep once again.

"Martin, Martin, wake up, Martin."

I forced my heavy eyes open, using every strength in my body to respond. "Uh."

"Get up; we're leaving now." My subconsciousness delivered me back into the same reality it once took me from. I watched as Tuma walked away.

I got up staggering around like a drunk man. Everyone was rushing to grab their stuff while I slowly walked over to JJ.

"Hey JJ, are we going back home?" I urged.

"I don't know, ask Tuma," he answered.

Tuma with her bag already packed with her stuff, helped Sophie get ready to leave. I quickly made my way over to her.

"Hey Tuma, are we heading back home?" I appeal.

"Mom said things don't look good back home, so we have to keep on moving," Tuma responded. I wanted to ask what was happening back home but I was afraid to.

An old Mandingo man stood at the front of the door; he had a machete attached to the belt on his waist. Story was that Mom helped save the man's son when he had a severe fever. He asked my mom if we were ready to go.

Everything was happening fast, it felt like a race with no ending. I picked up my small backpack and put it on my back. We were back on the road again trotting down the open road. The Mandingo man led us through a pathway into the forest. He cut down small obstacles that stood in his way. On each side of the narrow road was a plantation of cacao fruit trees. The cocoa fruit was ripe and ready to be picked. I wanted to pick one of them from the trees, but Mom rejected my request to do so. Beneath the thick skin of the cacao fruit was the cocoa beans covered with sweet citrus nectar. I thought about how back home I could just go to the marketplace, without asking for permission, and buy the citrus juice.

We heard a commotion not too far away from where we were. As we got closer, we could hear people arguing and screaming at each other. It was a group of people arguing with an older man who had a machete.

"What's going on?" my mother implored one of the bystanders.

"It's this man over here, he's blocking people from crossing the border," said a mid-age short Liberian man.

I felt like this was exactly what I've been waiting for. Now we really had no other option but to go back home. After fifteen minutes of waiting, my mother made her way up to the front to try to reason with the older man. Despite her attempt, he was reluctant to let anyone go by. Mom offered him some money, but he did not accept it. Twenty minutes turned to over five hours of trying to convince the old man to let us go by. A group of middle-aged men came running from behind him. "The soldiers said if we don't let their people cross over, they are going to come over here and bomb everything."

After receiving the news, the old man was gripped with fear. He grabbed his bag, and fled into town. Everyone began to rush past the gate, making their way to the river.

We came to a large body of water. Formed by several streams of water joining together to create this larger body. The waves from the current were rising up-and-down as if they were racing each other. A man in a canoe transported people from one side to the other. He took Sophie, Tuma, and JJ. He then made his way back to get the rest of us. I grabbed my bag and took the furthest seat in the front. Mom was afraid of water; she just wanted to get over to the other side. I was amazed by the majesty of the Cavalla River. It stretched so far it looked like it didn't have a beginning. I put my hand in the water to feel this great force of nature.

"What is this boy doing man? Put your hand back in the boat," Mom commanded.

"I just wanted to touch the water," I answered back.

"Do you know what can happen if this tips over?" she said, probably hoping I'd understand what she was insinuating.

I could see that she was petrified so I decided not to argue with her and kept quiet. She had somehow succeeded in destroying the experience. I was caught up in my own thoughts of frustration that I forgot to enjoy the signifance. It wasn't long till we got to the other side. I was surprised to see there were other Liberians there who also crossed over earlier during the day at some point. I saw lots of different faces and heard different languages. I've heard my Mom and Dad tell us a story about Liberia, but for the first time in my life, I was actually here. Sophie hugged Mom, Tuma, JJ and I. "Welcome to Liberia," one of the soldiers yelled out to the crowd of people who had crossed over the river.

I recognized a face amongst the crowd- a kid I used to know when I was in kindergarten, his name was Morris. He used to be one of the coolest kids in school. He was a few years older than me, so I secretly looked up to him at the time.

"Morris, Morris," I blurted, hoping to get his attention. He stopped and looked at me as if I had ten heads.

"Huh," he gestured, "do I know you?"

"Yes," I responded smiling back, "you and I went to school together remember?"

"No," he snarled glaring back at me, "I don't remember you."

He walked away from me not once looking back. I could have sworn he knew exactly who I was. I watched him as he disappeared into the crowd of people. I felt like I blew my only chance to become friends with the guy I looked up to. I stood there hoping perhaps maybe he would come back and talk to me.

"Martin," JJ called from behind me, "we are leaving now."

I could see he and the others had their stuff in hand and were ready to make the journey to the next town. I grabbed my backpack that was lying on the ground. I looked once more at the Cavalla River hoping to keep the image fresh in my mind. We walked for a while and stopped at a mud house in the forest. The people who lived there welcomed us.

The house was packed with tired people resting from the long journey. We sat down in the corner of the house that wasn't occupied. My Mom went over and talked to the owner of the house. She came back and said, "We can spend the night here."

"I'm hungry," I complained to her, holding my stomach.

She instructed us to fill a bowl with achecīr and then open a can of sardine to eat with it.

Tuma opened the bag, grabbed the bowl that was sitting on the top of the achecīr, and filled it to the top. She grabbed an unopened can of sardines and spread it over. She handed me the bowl to share with JJ and repeated the process for her and Sophie. That was our meal for the night.

As we were eating, eyes started glaring at us. I tried looking away because I knew we didn't have much. Mom saw two kids standing near me looking into the bowl. She saw that they want to eat, but I was being selfish.

"Call your friends over to eat," she interrupted.

"They're not my friends," I objected while stuffing another handful into my mouth.

"They are hungry just like you now call them over to eat," she said sternly.

"Ok. Come," I said to them.

They shyly approached and sat down making eye contact with me for my approval for them to start eating. I nodded my head, signaling it's okay. The four of us began to eat and the food slowly got smaller. I saw JJ eating a lot faster. I told him to slow down; the food's not going to run anywhere just like my Mom used to always tell me.

"Martin these kids are going to eat everything. You don't know when our next meal is. So if I were you, I would eat as much as I could," JJ protested in a low voice.

I followed his example and started eating fast. The

two boys eating with us saw what was going on and they started eating fast as well. When the food was gone, I was a little upset. Upset that my mother allowed strangers to eat our food, just like she always did back home. I went up to her and told her what had just happened.

"Don't worry there will always be food," she said, as she wiped the smudged remains from my mouth.

We got the bed ready and settled in for the night. A gunshot woke some people from their sleep and panic spread throughout the building. The packed living room started to become chaotic. I didn't hear the gunshot; I was in a deep sleep. Mom woke us up and left to find out what was going on. I was very confused as a rumor circulated around that the area was not safe. After a while, she came back and said, "pack your bags we can't spend the night in this place. We have to go to the next town."

Once again we started walking, I was tired and irritated. The random sounds of the jungle scared me. I feared that a wild animal would attack us before getting to a safe place. It was gloomy and dark out, and the walk felt like forever. The only light we had was a single flashlight. With each step, I felt my feet aching. I was afraid of complaining because I didn't want to know that they were in pain.

After a few hours of walking nonstop, we came to a stop at a nearby village that was hidden in the woods. We were able to spend the night there. In the morning I asked my Mom if I could go with the other village boys into the forest to see where they got their water from. "Okay," she said, raising her voice a little louder as I started to head towards them, "don't spend too much time, we're going to be leaving soon."

I quickly ran off with the boys, joining their routine. We made our way into the thick jungle. There was a trail going uphill, clusters of tree vines invading the path. "Hey wait up!" I yelled out making my way to where they were, and trying to catch my breath at the same time. We came to a small creek that flowed down the mountain. The water was bright and refreshing. They dropped their buckets in and scooped up the water that was caught in it. After scooping the water, we turned around and started making our way back down. I felt accomplished when we reached the village. I told my Mom about the hill and the creek water.

As the sun began rising high over the morning sky, my Mom told the people of the village that we had a place we needed to get to not too far from there so we will be leaving soon. They gave us water and extra food for the journey. They bid us farewell and sent us on our way.

"I want to come back and visit after everything is settled," I told my Mom hoping to provoke a positive reaction.

"That's fine with me," she said smiling at me. "When you graduate from school."

When she said that, I knew it wasn't going to happen anytime soon. I thought about telling her that I lost my teacher's book but I figure she already had enough to think about. JJ was quiet and as usual, Mom and Tuma talked about where we were going next. After walking for a short time, we saw a farmer who looked like he was heading into town, the same direction we were going.

"Sir!" Tuma yelled, hoping to get his attention. "What town are you heading to?"

The man stopped and looked at us. "The town near here is Webo," he responded.

"Tuma, ask him how far away we are," I whispered.

"Excuse me, sir," she yelled, "how far away are we from this town?" Tuma asked.

"Not too far away."

We followed him and not too long afterward; we emerged out of the jungle onto a dusty and dirty road similar to the ones back home. The man walked faster and left us behind. Mom saw a house a mile down from where we were. The house was similar to the ones back home, except this one was much older. It seemed the owner did not spend a lot of time fixing it up. Mom knocked on the door, but no one answered. As we were about to leave, a tall Liberian woman opened the door slightly, barely revealing her face.

"Hello, can I help you?"

"Yeah, we were wondering if we can stay here before making our journey to Kahnwia Camp tomorrow," Mom asked hoping to get a good response.

"Hold on," requested the lady behind the door, "let me go ask my husband." After about 10 minutes the lady came back.

"I'm sorry, but we don't have enough space, we would let you stay otherwise." she said with pity evident in her voice.

"Wait, I know that voice," proclaimed Mom out loud, "It's me, Sis. Linda." Mom said, raising her voice "You used to rent from me, back in Grabo you and your boyfriend." The lady opened the door to get a good look at who was talking.

"Linda!" She made her way over to hug Mom. "Please come inside," she begged her, "what brings you here?"

"There were rumors of rebels coming to Grabo, so we fled for safety, but we will be heading back soon," my mom responded.

"Yeah because I know you have a lot of houses back home and you're running a successful business, anything I can do for you?"

"My kids and I just need a place to rest for the night before making our journey to Kahnwia Camp tomorrow." My mom requested.

"We have plenty of space; we have two rooms that are unoccupied. Make yourselves at home; we will be eating later so I'll make sure to cook more food."

This woman and her boyfriend used to always be late on their rent. Yet, my mother would always give them a grace period to pay. Now she was being gracious to my mother and returning the favor.

I asked my Mom, "Why did the lady lie about not having room?"

"Well, she did that because this town is not the safest town. People can do harm to you for no reason," Mom explained.

"Was that why the farmer from yesterday left us behind to go into town?" I questioned.

"That's exactly right," she reasoned.

That night the lady prepared a big meal for us, she filled big bowls with rice and soup. Mom, Tuma, JJ, Sophie and I all ate from the same bowl. The lady and her husband ate separately. Instead of savoring and enjoying each bite I ate fast as if it was my last meal. My mother looked at me, but this time, she didn't say anything. That night we went to sleep, I laid in bed with my eyes open. I was afraid to shut them because I felt like at any moment we would have to start walking again. Thoughts of the day before kept me awake. No matter how hard I tried, I couldn't push them out of my head. Once again my eyes got heavy, and I was overtaken by my subconscious.

Chapter 7

The crowing of roosters woke me from my light sleep. I got up and walked near the window, to look out and see if the people of the town were up and about. The town was quiet except for the sound the roosters made. I carefully made way to the back door trying not to step on the others sleeping. The cool morning breeze rushed in as I gently slipped out the door, trying not to make a noise. The breeze traveled through my short curly hair, the sensation distracting me from thinking about the long journey ahead. I stood by the small kitchen area away from the street trying to avoid being seen by the local people. Not long afterward everybody else woke up. The lady made us breakfast from the leftover dinner that we ate the previous night. After eating, Tuma insisted on washing the dishes. The woman refused because it was one of the few things she enjoyed doing around the house to keep her busy. We packed our stuff, filled up a few jugs of water and packed some food for the voyage. The thought of a long journey sickened me. I managed to keep the blisters off my feet, but this time, I was bound to get some just like Mom and the others. We were back on the road again, and I feared to ask how long it will take till we get to the next town. The hot sun was starting to rise over the horizon. A little while into the journey we all started sweating. Tuma requested that we take a break. We set our bags down, and Mom passed a jug of water to drink from. We talked about our new home, how it was going to look and who would get the biggest room and so forth. We laughed and argued over rooms. All of a sudden, we were interrupted by a loud sound that seemed to be approaching very fast. We quickly grabbed our bags and started running to find a safe place to hide. JJ looking behind saw that it was a semi-trailer truck approaching.

"It's a big truck coming," JJ explained pointing at the fast approaching diesel guzzling giant.

We all looked back, and a sense of relief came over us. We slowed down and started walking again.

"One of my aunt's sons drives those trucks," Mom implored while staring back at the truck. "O God please let it be him."

JJ started waving the truck man down. We followed his lead as the truck man got closer. He stared at us as he passed by, then slammed on the brakes as if something struck him. The truck slowly came to a complete stop; we quickly began to make our way towards it.

I feared that he might change his mind and drive off. So I ran in front of everyone else. I reached out my small arms to grab the door that seemed so far away. I heard laughter from the back as they all approached. JJ reached over me and pulled open the truck door flinging the door and me with it. Mom went in. A big smile lit up on the driver's face, he instantly knew who she was. They exchanged greetings and started talking, catching up on each other's' life. There were two back seats and behind the backseat was a cabin, where JJ and Tuma sat while Mom, Sophie and I sat in the front seat. The ride was filled with conversations between Mom and the truck driver. I sensed that they were fascinated with the different buttons in the truck. I was curious as to how it was possible for one man to drive such a colossal machine.

Not too long into the ride, JJ and Tuma fell asleep. Sophie was still up, and Mom was still having a conversation with her cousin the truck driver. We passed by many plantations, and we also saw a bus filled with passengers that broke down on the side of the road. We saw a big green snake crossing the road which we had a privilege of running over. A few miles on the road, we saw a strange man squatting on the side of the road watching us go by. He had no shirt on, a flap of cloth covered his private. He had an intense gaze on his face and in his hand, he held a machete. "Who is that?" I asked mom, pointing at the strange man.

"That is what we call a bushman," she answered, looking in the direction I was pointing.

"What is he doing?" I inquired, curious to find out.

"He's waiting for the people to walk by so he can get money from them," added my mom's cousin.

I started to think about the people we passed who were also making the journey by foot, worrying for their safety. I started to think what would happen if we were in their position. What if he decided to kill each of us? Those thoughts scared me, so I tried to distract myself by listening to Mom and the truck driver talk. I didn't understand what their conversation was about, but they were both very engaged on the topic. I looked at Sophie, and she was already asleep. I yawned and not long afterward it was lights out.

When I woke up from my long nap to my surprise, everyone else was up. The truck driver was still driving, he and Mom were still talking. I closed my eyes again, but this time, it was harder to fall back asleep. I quietly listen to the sound of the engine laboring, the loud tires against the gravel ground, and the sound of the back tires bouncing up and down from the small grooves on the road. It was in this repetition that I felt like there was no end to our journey. To my surprise, the truck began to decelerate slowly and came to a stop. The dust lifted from the tires had completely blocked the view.

"Okay this is it," blurted the truck driver.

"Mom where are we?" I asked curiously.

She didn't answer my question, as she was still caught up in the conversation. JJ stared at me with a blank look while sucking on his thumb like a baby. I never understood why he always did that, but it was just his thing.

"Thank you very much, you really did well for us," Mom said to her cousin the truck driver. We all got down one by one. The dust settled and things cleared up, I could see it was a small town. It wasn't like any city I've ever seen before, I wanted to get back in the truck, but it was too late. He was already reversing his engine and right on his way. We made our way up the hill where people were, vendors were selling their products. My mother asked them if they knew a particular person by the name of Victor Toe. All the people we asked that question to said no, so we kept on walking. We came across this peculiar fellow who seemed jubilant.

Mom questioned him, "Sir, do you know Victor Toe?" He looked at us as if we all had two heads. "Where are you from?" he requested, hoping to find out who we were.

"We are from Ivory Coast just visiting," Mom replied.

"Visitors! Come, come," he said. We started following him not knowing where he was leading us to. After walking in between a few houses, we came to a beat up cement plastered house with one entrance door. The roof was old; the zinc was rusting and needed to be replaced.

"This is Victor's place," proclaimed the man, smiling at us.

"Thank you," Mom said to the fellow.

"Knock knock," Mom greeted as she entered the house.

There was a young man in his early 20's sitting down holding a baby in his hand. He looked familiar, but I couldn't tell where I'd seen him before. My Mom called out to him. He instantly knew who she was.

"Hi Aunty," he responded as he got up to greet her.

"Wow little man is big now," he put in staring at me. "Who's the other one?" he asked.

"That's Sophie, she wasn't born yet when you left," Mom explained.

He quickly gravitated to her, and asked her "how are you doing?"

Sophie shyly disappeared behind Tuma, hoping to avoid the stranger.

"Where is Victor?" Mom requested.

"Victor went to Tiehnpo; he will be back either tomorrow or the day after."

We sat our stuff down and looked for a place to sit.

"Offer us some water, my man, we came a long way," my mother requested.

"Oh, aunty I'm sorry, hold on let me get you people some water."

He rushed out of the house with the little baby and disappeared in the back of the house. He then came back with a young lady holding two cups of water in her hand. She gave one cup to Mom and handed the other cup to Tuma. She then went to the back of the house and grabbed another cup. She gave it to JJ who then asked me if I wanted to drink first. With no hesitation, I grabbed the cup and started drinking away.

"Save some for me," JJ muttered grabbing the cup.

"There's more water where that came from," the young guy interjected while giggling.

"So who is the Madame?" Mom urged the young gentleman.

"O aunty this is my wife," he answered.

The young lady greeted my Mom and then soon after she left without excusing herself.

"Why did your Madame just leave?" Mom questioned.

"Oh, she just went to prepare a meal for you guys," he uttered in a mumbling voice.

It seemed like he had a reverence for Mom. I didn't understand why but later on during the day I would find out.

It was dinner time, and the young man's wife had prepared an excellent meal for us. Sophie, Mom, and Tuma ate together. While JJ, the young man and I ate together. His wife stayed in the kitchen and cooked making sure that we didn't run out of food. My mother called her over to come and eat, but she insisted on staying in the kitchen.

The young man looked at me and questioned, "Do you remember me?"

"No I don't think so," I answered back.

He chuckled and said, "I used to beat your butt when you were a baby."

I didn't know how I felt about the whole situation. Part of me wanted to ask why he did that but the other side of me did not want to find out.

"Is my dad from here?" I asked the young guy, curious to know.

"Yeah, your dad is from Tiehnpo where your uncle Victor is right now, that's where all your tribal people are." he claimed excitingly looking straight me.

My speculation became filled with wonders. My mind became flooded with anticipation. I was curious, and I wanted to know more about the people of Tiehnpo. I didn't know I had more family members apart from the ones I already knew.

"Who is Victor?" I asserted, leaning in to learn more.

"Victor is your father's youngest brother," answered the young guy, "If it weren't for him, I wouldn't have a place to stay."

"Victor sounds like a good man," I added.

"Yes he is," agreed the young man.

After the meal, I went to go see Mom, I asked her what we were going to do next.

"I'm looking to see if I can find a car that's heading to Zwedru tonight," said Mom, "if anything … We will spend the night here, early in the morning we'll find a car heading to Zwedru."

At first, I hated the small town but knowing that not far from here laid the community where my ancestors resided made me feel more at home.

Tonight was dark, so dark that it was hard to see what stands ten feet in front of us. I stared outside the door at the lonely sky that was filled with dark clouds. I wanted to see the stars; I wanted to see the moon shining bright and lighting the dark night just like back home. Out of the dark street, I saw a figure appear, it became closer and closer. I quickly made my way back inside the house, scared that it could be someone else trying to harm me. Surprisingly it was my Mom, she entered the house. She then looked around and saw that everyone was getting ready to go to sleep.

"Pack your bags we're leaving tonight," she repeated, "hurry up, the driver is waiting for us. Other people are going to Zwedru tonight."

Once again we packed our stuff as fast as we could.

We thanked the young guy for being kind to us and for treating us with hospitality. It was a bittersweet feeling like part of me wanted to stay and hear more about my ancestors. Another part of me wanted to continue because the town was too small for a city boy like myself.

That night, we unloaded our luggage in the back of a pickup truck. My mother sat in the passenger seat while JJ, Tuma, Sophie and I sat in the bed of the truck. Tuma hugged onto Sophie and JJ did the same to me.

"Let go," I lamented to him forcing myself from his grip. The truck was packed with other people who were traveling to Zwedru and nearby towns. The people were charismatic, not like the ones from back home. It was a different culture; they were interesting people, and I felt as if I could grow accustomed to their ways.

After driving for a while, there was a commotion. I heard people talking amongst themselves about the corruption that was taking place within the government and making jokes about Zwedru. I thought about how it didn't compare to its former glory.

I asked the lady next to me, "Is this Zwedru."

"Yeah, it is, we'll soon be in town," she kindly responded back.

"Thank you," I said to her.

"No problem dear," she replied.

Not long afterward, we came to the junction where people who were going to Zwedru were getting off. It was in the middle of the night; we had no place to stay and we knew nobody. We went across the street and knocked on the first door. A gentleman opened the door.

"Hi, can I help you?" he requested.

"Yeah, my kids and I need a place to stay for tonight," Mom begged remorsefully.

"I'm sorry," responded the man, "I only have one bedroom."

"We'll take it," Mom answered. "I'll give you some money only for tonight, tomorrow morning we'll be looking for our own place."

"Okay," agreed the man.

He walked us into a dark room, with no lights. The only light we had was the moonlight that barely came in through the small window. We all piled onto the single mattress that we had been carrying the whole way. I tried to sleep and even though my family members were close, the darkness had a grip on me. I extended my hand in the dark to touch everybody to make sure they were all there.

"What are you doing," Tuma commanded.

"Nothing," I replied back.

Silence filled the air; I could tell everyone was on the brink of falling asleep. A gunshot fired and we all started to panic.

"Everybody get down, get on the ground right now," Mom said.

We all got off the bed and lied down on the ground, waiting. Another round was fired, this time it sounded like it was closer. Tuma started crying.

"Everybody be quiet," Mom commanded.

This was my first time hearing Tuma cry. I couldn't hold it in, so I started laughing. Mom started getting upset.

"Oh God, what is this boy trying to do to us," she said, disturbed.

It just made the whole situation even funnier. I started laughing even harder while trying to hold back my laughter. Then from nowhere I heard a thump in the back of my head. "Ouch, who did that?" I questioned, almost tearing up.

"I'm not getting killed because of you now shut up," whispered JJ, who was close to impossible to see in the dark.

After a while, Mom felt like it was safe to get back on the bed. We got back in our spots; I knew we were all there but this time we were all gripped with fear. The next day, we packed our bags and Mom gave the gentleman some money. We headed out in search of a new place to call home.

Chapter 8

My mother heard that the U.N was in town. She was friends with some of their workers so she decided to go and find where they were staying to ask them about how her property and assets were. It was a three-mile walk to where the U.N camp was located.

When we got to the camp, there were tents pitched up everywhere. There was countless number of people stationed everywhere refugees who had lost all they had because of war. I saw hurting people everywhere. I saw mothers holding babies whose body were dry. My heart became filled with compassion and I wanted to help. I went to the fellow who was helping the people.

"Excuse me, sir, how can I help?" I asked, smiling at him.

"Can you measure?" he muttered back.

I felt shameful because I didn't know how to measure. He then went back to work, and from there I knew my help was not needed. I walked away and went back to where my Mom was. She and her friend was engaged in a conversation. I sat by there patiently waiting to be instructed on what to do next. Sophie and Tuma had gone together to find a place for us to stay. JJ sat ten feet away from me waiting for Mom to finish up her conversation so that we could leave. After talking to the guy for a while, she then came over.

"I need you guys to go and find Tuma and Sophie at the new place," Mom requested, "go back the same way we came from but this time stay on the road and go all the way down until you see one of the last houses."

"Okay," I answered, "when are you going to come home?"

"I'll come home later don't worry about me," she assured smiling at us.

JJ and I got up and started racing back to town. We passed through the bush roads into a small town on the outskirts of the city. On the side of the road was a bee's nest. It was dripping with honey, but was also swamped by a bunch of bees.

"Hey Martin go get the honey from the bees' nest," suggested JJ, testing me to see if I actually would.

"Is it safe?" I inquired, curiously.

"Yeah, it's not going to do anything," he said, trying to keep a straight face.

I carefully approach the nest hoping to snag some honey without being stung. As I was about to make my final attempt to grab some honey, JJ screamed, "Martin what are you doing, are you trying to kill yourself?"

"No what do you mean, I'm just trying to get some honey," I quickly responded back.

"If those bees sting you, you'll die right here," he gloated sternly.

I slowly backed away from them bees nest and made my way back to him. I never thought that I could die from many bee stings. The thought of death gripped me, I thought about death the whole walk back. We walked on the dirt road until we finally got onto the paved roads. From there we made our way through the town.

Down the lonely road, a stranger was approaching from the direction we were heading towards. As the figure got closer, I could tell it was a man. It was a tall man wearing sweatpants and a plain T-shirt.

"Martin it's your dad," proclaimed JJ, excitingly. JJ, started to run towards him. I was staring at my father in disbelief. It made no sense to me, how could my father just come out of nowhere? I was tired and fatigued and had no strength in me to run. As I got closer, I could make out the face, a face that I used to see so long ago. His scruffy beard and new gray hair reminded me of the time that has passed since I last saw him.

"My own son is not happy to see me," stated dad. I used the last ounce of energy; I had in my body to make an effort to run towards him. When I finally reached him, I embraced him.

"Are you okay?" he asked.

I nodded my head up and down.

"Some people were telling me that you guys were in town, so I came looking for you," he declared. "I miss you guys; I'm so glad that you guys are okay." He let go of us and asked, "Where is your mother?"

JJ answered, "she's at the U.N camp finding out some stuff about back home."

"Okay, this is what I'm gonna do for you guys," he added, "I'm going to give you some money for food. I have some things to take care of, but I will come see you guys again okay?"

"Okay," JJ answered smiling.

He was more excited to see dad than I was. He handed us some Liberian currency. He hugged us one more time then kissed me on the forehead. He then went on his way, and we continued the way we were heading.

"Wasn't that nice seeing your dad?" JJ insisted, hoping to provoke a response from me.

"Yeah I guess," I responded back.

"You didn't seem happy to see him," he replied leaning in.

I didn't have anything to say, so I kept quiet.

"You should be grateful you know, at least you have a dad that loves you," JJ answered for me.

I thought about the years that he was in and out of my life. It felt like in my whole life he wasn't there. I wanted to ask JJ about his father. Since he was the only one asking all the questions.

"What about your father?"

"I don't really know my father," he said looking down, "only my grandparents they're the ones who took care of me."

I was cut deep to the heart. I tried to think of something to say to comfort him, but there was nothing. We walked in silence the rest of the way. We walked past our destination, and went further down the road. We realized there weren't any more houses down there so we quickly turned around and started making our way back. As we were going back, I looked down a hill where a brick house was located. Outside the brick house was a little girl who looked just like Sophie.

I called out, "Sophie!" She looked in our direction, a sign that she heard her name. JJ and I quickly made our way down the hill to where she was. I hugged her and asked where Tuma was. She pointed inside the house. JJ and I entered the brick house, the temperature dropping significantly. Upon entering, we were greeted by the wife of the owner. It was a three bedroom house with a large living room. There was no electricity, and there was an empty indoor chicken coop. They had a lot of chicken running around. Tuma was arranging Mom's room. She set up the mosquito net, and she laid down the mattress underneath it.

"Tuma!" I called out.

"I see you guys found the place," she uttered.

"Yeah we did," added JJ, "we also found Martin's dad."

"Oh wow congratulations," she answered, "I hope he's doing good."

She didn't seem at all that interested in talking about dad. She quickly went back to what she was doing. JJ and I stood there waiting for her to give us instruction. "What are you guys doing here? Go play or something," she addressed.

The owners of the house had two kids. A young girl about my age, and a boy who was about JJ's age. They were friendly, respectful and well trained by their parents to respect people. JJ and I approached the boy and told him that we had some money and we wanted to spend it on food.

The boy responded, "the places down on the main street are the only good places for food, but there is a Kool-aid place right up to the road from here."

"What is kool-aid?" I inquired.

"It's like yahwu," said JJ. (Yahwu is a type of kool-aid made from different types of plants.)

"Let's go get it," I blurted excitedly.

We ran down to the corner store. There was a young man in the small booth who seemed to be distracted by a device in his hand which he hid away when he saw us.

"How can I help you," he requested looking at each of us.

"We would like to buy one Kool-Aid," I suggested to him.

"All right, one Kool-Aid coming up, that will be one dollar," he said, during the exchange.

He handed me the Kool-Aid, and I gave him the dollar bill. As soon as he did, we ran back home. When we got back home, we filled up a cup of water and then opened the Kool-Aid pack and put it inside the water. We all took turns stirring it until it completely dissolved in the water.

"Okay, now try it," the boy announced.

I took a sip, and my taste buds caught on fire. It was one of the greatest things I've ever tasted. I've lived in the city practically my whole life and I've tried different types of soft drinks and juices, but this was different. We ended up going back and buying a second pack because JJ wanted one too.

Later on during the day Mom came home. She brought food for all of us including the family whose house we were staying at. We all ate until we were satisfied. As I ate I thought about the refugees I saw earlier today. I wanted to bring my food to them, but I knew Mom wouldn't let me walk the streets of Zwedru by myself. As the sun went down the moon began to shine brightly. The constellations decorated the night sky. Two oil lamps were lit in the room Mom, Sophie and I were staying in. That night we all slept, there were no gunshots. We slept great that night. It finally felt like things were coming together.

Chapter 9

That next morning, the scorching sun rays penetrated the window, lighting up the room. I tried to fight the urge to wake up, but it was just too hot. My eyes opened and I looked around, Mom was nowhere to be found. On the other side of the bed laid Sophie who always somehow managed to be facing the wrong side of the bed in the morning. I heard voices from the outside, so I peeked through the small cracked window. It was the wife of the house, her daughter, and Tuma cooking breakfast. I looked around hoping maybe JJ would be sitting around getting ready to eat. Yet the woman's husband and her son were nowhere around, JJ was also not around. I jumped out of bed, put on my shoes and went out to investigate.

"Good morning Tuma, good morning auntie," I said.

"Good morning Martin," Tuma answered back.

"Good morning sweetheart," the owner's wife added.

"Do you know where Mom and JJ are?" I requested.

The wife of the house responded, "JJ went with my husband and my son to go get her some log to finish up the kitchen, your mother went to go talk to some friends about work."

"Okay thank you," I said smiling at her while trying to avoid eye contact with her daughter.

"The food should be ready soon," Tuma added in.

I knew the day wasn't going to be as fun as I wished it would. I couldn't believe they would just leave me behind and go get wood. I walked back inside the cool brick house and sat down in one of the vine chairs. I thought about home and about dad coming home with us. I imagined him and Mom talking things through and falling in love again. I imagined him teaching me new things. These thoughts would always come to my mind. I would usually dismiss them, but I chose to entertain them this time.

"Martin the food is ready, wake up your sister!" Tuma reckoned, as her voice echoed through the whole house.

I went to go wake up Sophie, but she was already up staring at me. Smiling, like she always did whenever I was sent to wake her up back home.

"Let's go, Tuma said it's time to eat," I said to her.

She pretended to go back to sleep. I didn't want to be yelled at for not waking her up. So I went over and started making jokes to try to see if she would smile and laugh. She resisted but finally she started laughing.

"Let's go, all the food is going to be gone," I explained urgently.

She got up from the bed, and I grabbed her hand and lead her towards the door and down the hallway that went outside.

"Shoes," requested said.

I looked back in the room and saw her flip flops on the side of the bed. I ran back and grabbed them for her. We rushed through the hallway to get outside and then to the kitchen. As we were going to the kitchen, we saw JJ, the owner of the house and his son. They had just gotten back from cutting logs in the woods. They were drenched in sweat, and they seemed happy to be home. I swiftly made my way into the kitchen with Sophie. I grabbed my plate that Tuma had already prepared beforehand. Sophie joined Tuma and the girls to eat together.

JJ entered the vicinity and declared, "where is my food?"

Tuma responded, "maybe next time before you go somewhere you'll let me know so we can keep your food."

I saw JJ eyes began to swell up with tears. He just came back from a long day of work just to find out that he wasn't going to be eating. The owner of the house offered to give JJ his portion, but Tuma refused and said that he needed to learn his lesson. I wanted to tell him that it was just a joke that his food was right in the corner but it was too good to be true. I couldn't believe the toughest guy that I knew was actually crying over food.

"JJ I'm playing, your food is right in the corner," Tuma finally said.

It was too late; she had emasculated him. He refused to eat the food, so I offered to eat the food for him. His face showed more anger at my offer.

"Martin if you touch that food I'll beat you," Tuma said sternly.

The bowl of food sat in the corner even after we were

all done eating. After everyone had left the kitchen, the bowl of food disappeared. No one knew what happened to the food. When we asked JJ, he would just shrug his shoulders.

"Hey, Martin wasn't your dad supposed to come get you today?" Tuma inquired.

I thought to myself I didn't even know he was supposed to come get me.

"Did he say he was going to come get me?" I questioned her.

"I think so, that's what he said the other day," she implored trying to recollect.

"Maybe he had some important business to take care of," I suggested hoping she would drop the conversation.

"Yeah, like he did for the past few years, never being there for his children," Tuma replied attacking him.

"At least he gives us some money," I proposed defending my old man.

She laughed and then went back to what she was doing. This instantly made me bitter. Another lie, another promise not kept. What type of father is this? I wanted to cry, but I held it in.

JJ looked at me and said, "Martin don't listen to her, she's just trying to be mean." JJ and I sat in the living room frowning at the wall. The owners of the house's son tried to comfort us, but we told him to leave us alone. We then started talking about moving out even though both of us were not old enough to do such a thing. Somehow this made us feel better, the idea of escaping Tuma's meanness. We spent the whole day inside waiting until Mom came home to tell on Tuma. Tuma knew what we were going to do, so she tried to make a deal with us. We both turned down the deal to rat on her.

When Mom came home later that day she was tired. She just wanted to eat and go to sleep. She didn't want to hear any complaints. JJ approached me and said, "go tell Mom what Tuma did.

"Maybe we should wait for tomorrow?" I suggested.

"No, tomorrow she might not be home again," he argued.

"You're right okay," I said.

"Mom …," I stated in a low voice approaching her near the kitchen as she ate her food and talked with the wife of the house and Tuma.

"What is it MacMartin?" she proclaimed in the nickname she'd always call me.

"Mom, today Tuma was mean to JJ and me. She didn't give JJ food, and she said that my dad is a whacked man." I reported pausing afterward, to hear Tuma get the ultimate rebuke of her lifetime. But instead, that wasn't what happened. It seemed that night that the odds were against us. She didn't ask about the situation, she just said sorry and asked if JJ still needed food, which he declined. I walked back inside the house and sat on the vine chair., looking at the one candle that illuminated the room. JJ and I felt betrayed by our own mother. We thought of ways to get even but we were also afraid of getting reprimanded by Mom, so we decided to let it go. He and I talked until we both fell asleep on the couch.

I woke up the next morning, and I was laying under

the mosquito net that surrounds the bed. I was able to catch Mom before she left to go into the marketplace.

"Mom, where are you going, can I come?" I asked.

"No, you can't come with me, I'll be back later on during the day but your dad is supposed to come pick you up today," she proposed back to me.

"How do I even know he's going to come get me, he didn't show up yesterday. I don't think I want to see him," I said frowning.

"Who said he was coming to get you yesterday, he was in Monrovia yesterday," she interjected.

"Tuma told me that," I murmured, feeling betrayed.

"Well Tuma must have misheard," she said. "Now go get ready, he could be here anytime."

I felt like everyone was playing with my emotions. I didn't know who to trust anymore. The thought of seeing my dad and spending time with him didn't seem appealing to me, now that I didn't know what to think of him. Mom stepped out and went on her way, I followed her outside hoping maybe she would change her mind and say that I could come along. I watched her as she disappeared into the distance where my eyes could not trail her anymore.

Tuma called to me to come shower. She boiled the hot water on the fire and dumped it in a bucket filled with half full cold water. She grabbed my hand, the bucket of hot water, a bar of soap the scrubber and lead me to the bathroom. She poured water on me, then put soap on the sponge and washed me down. Afterward, she rinsed me with the hot water, dried me down with a towel, and put my favorite pair of clothes on me. I went into the living room and sat down, contemplating what the day would be like with dad and how our conversation would go. The wait felt like forever, JJ had gone into the forest again to help get wood with the owner of the house and his son. This time, he told Tuma where he was going.

I heard a vehicle outside, so I rushed towards the front door to see who it was. Getting out of the passenger seat was the same familiar face I saw a few days ago. I wanted to run out and greet him; but I didn't want him to think all the time he left Mom, Sophie and I were put behind us. I went back and sat in the living room waiting for Tuma to call out to me. I heard the truck ride away and I thought to myself, what if he just left again? My head became filled with negative thoughts clouding my ability to reason. I tried, but I couldn't dismiss them.

"Martin!" Tuma called out.

I took my time, making my way through the living room door and then through the hallway. I took a left turn towards the smaller hallway that went outside but waited for a few moments before going out. Tuma had a smile on her face, the wife of the house pretended as if she minded her business.

"Wow," my dad exclaimed, "are you ready to spend some time with me?"

I nodded my head up and down; I walked towards him, and we both said goodbye to Tuma and the wife of the house. I wasn't sure where he was bringing me, but I was happy he came for me. I didn't know what to say, but I was open to having any conversation.

Chapter 10

We walked along the cracked sidewalk that stretched down for miles leading to the downtown.

I asked him, "where is the truck that you came in?"

"The truck belonged to my friend I just asked him to drop me off here."

"Oh okay," I replied disappointingly.

He started to point out some of the historical places. He told me the great people that once came to those places. I was amazed by how much he knew about Zwedru. I wanted to be as knowledgeable as him to be able to point out different places and tell their histories. Along the way passed an older man in a booth exchanging currencies. Beside his booth sat a homeless man begging people walking by for money.

"Don't look at him," dad warned, "he might come after us asking for money again."

I figured the homeless man had already received money from my dad. I still wanted to stare at him, but I was afraid that my dad would say something else.

Downtown was packed with people walking up

and down the streets. Motorcycles weaved through the crowds and large vehicles carried cargo and people. For some reason, dad had a presence in town and the people recognized him. He introduced me to everyone we walked by, and they all said hi to me and welcomed me to Liberia. I felt accepted and loved, I finally belonged.

We entered a small shop. It had tables decorated with silverware. Busy waitresses ran back and forth getting orders. In the back corner was a bar area where adults ordered a drink and talked. It was a different environment from what I've been used to. My dad quickly called to one of the waitresses, she sat us down at a table and gave us a menu.

"What do you want to eat?" he asked me.

I looked at the menu, but I could not make out the words. *'Those days of skipping classes and not showing up for school were really paying off this time,'* I sarcastically thought to myself. I was silent and didn't say a thing.

"What about palm butter rice?" he suggested. This was his favorite food Mom used to make for him. I nodded my head up and down, in agreement with his suggestion.

"Okay I will get you that," he said back.

The waitress took down the order, then rushed back to the kitchen to fetch a bowl of palm butter rice. My dad started a small conversation by asking me how everyone was doing. The conversation went on for ten minutes or so until the waitress brought the food. I started to eat the palm butter rice. It was thick and not as good as Tuma's, but it had meat and dried fish in it those are two things that I really like. Our small talk then turned into a much deeper talk.

"Look Martin I'm asking you to forgive me for what I've done to you, your Mom and Sophie," dad requested sorrowfully.

I lost my appetite. The moment in time that I waited for finally arrived. I was lost for words; I did not know how to respond. I didn't want to speak for Mom or Sophie, but I knew that I could find space for forgiveness in my heart.

"I forgive you, Dad," I said while trying to swallow the rice I just chewed, "but you're going to have to talk to Mom and Sophie because I don't know how they feel."

He was relieved and was excited that I accepted his apologies. He had a look of disbelief on his face, a look of shock and surprise.

"Martin thank you, you don't know how much this means to me," he replied, tears resting on the corners of his eyes.

We talked some more, I was able to ask him a lot of questions. The waitress came back over and gave the receipt to dad. I thanked Dad for the food which he smiled at me and then we walked off.

"Where do you live dad?" I inquired.

"You won't be able to see my house tonight because it's late and I have to get you home," he explained, "but I live two blocks away from here. It's behind the government buildings. I work right on this street for the government. I'll be able to show you another time."

It was dark out, and the street lights did not illuminate all of downtown. We went over to a shop where one of

Dad's friend worked. It was late in the evening, so the man was closing up shop. Dad approached the man in a friendly manner.

"Hey my man, how are you doing?" asked dad, smiling at the fellow.

"I'm doing well, just closing shop," the man replied in a hurry.

"Man, I need you to help me with something?" dad said.

"Augustine, I can't do it right now, I have to get home to my family," the man said.

"My son too needs to get back home to his mother, and I don't want him to walk in the dark," dad argued.

The man looked at me and pondered for a moment. Then he told us to get in the car, dad and I sat in the front seat of the pickup truck. What felt like a long walk was only a few minutes ride down the street. Dad dropped me off and told me that he would come get me again so that I can come and see where he lived and also see where he worked. He also wanted me to meet his boss who was Head of Secretary for Zwedru. That night I explained to JJ about everything, I even told him that dad wanted to put us in school. I was excited, but JJ wasn't happy about the school part. Just like me he'd skipped classes and couldn't read. On top of that, he didn't like to be made fun of. I told Mom about everything; then I told Sophie and Tuma. I couldn't think of a better way to end the day.

Chapter 11

Days went by and things began to get better again. Mom had started her business and was making money. When the owner of the house, his son and JJ went out to the farm, I accompanied them. Dad came by and visited on many different occasions. He and Mom talked about putting Sophie and I in school.

We took a tour of the school. It was an old cemented concrete building that stretched a couple of hundred yards. Across the building was a newer building in which the older kids attended classes. Across from the school was a barrack where they kept prisoners. Soldiers would set outside the brick with their guns, talking amongst themselves and watching over the school. In the back of the school was what looked like an old rice plantation field. After dad walked Sophie and I around the school campus, he then brought us into the principal's office. There we greeted an old man with a bald head, wearing thick glasses. He and dad talked while Sophie and I walked around looking and touching everything that we saw. Afterward, Dad and the old man shook hands. We walk down to where my class would be, but didn't want to enter into the class because the teacher was in the middle of a lesson.

The man teaching asked my father, "can I help you?"

"Yes," my dad said surprisingly, "this is my son Martin, and he will be your new student."

That moment I felt a weird feeling in my stomach. The whole class looked at me; Sophie hid behind dad. The teacher walked over and shook my hand.

"Welcome to my class Martin, I look forward to teaching you," he said in an intellectual tone.

"Thank you sir," I responded back.

"Now if you'll excuse me I have to get back to teaching," he requested, before walking back.

"Thank you for your time sir," dad added.

We walked out of the class, and we made our way back home where we stayed.

"Your teacher seems like a nice guy," dad considered.

"Yes, I guess," I responded.

"What do you mean I guess?" he asked curiously.

"I mean … I don't know him, maybe after my first week or so I can tell you what I really think about him," I argued back.

"My man you're smart," he stated smiling at me.

He looked down at Sophie and smiled at her. I walked in front of them trying to lead the way. A thought came to my mind; I remembered one of my step-brothers also lived in Liberia.

"Dad do you know where Geoffrey is?" I asked.

"Geoffrey, yeah the man lives right in town here,

he actually lives right along the road," he said trying to remember.

I was overcome with excitement, the thought of seeing my big brother again was overwhelming. I started to jump up and down.

"Can we go see him please?" I suggested dad.

"I don't know. Your mom told me to bring you guys home soon," he argued.

"Please daddy," Sophie requested in her little voice.

It was too much for even my dad to say no. "All right we can go visit him only for just a little bit; then I have to bring you guys back home." I tried to keep the excitement in, but I just couldn't it was too much. When we got on the main road, I remembered the building across the road.

"Dad that's the building we stayed in when we came here the first night," I said reminiscing.

"Well Geoffrey's house is right across on this side of the street," he said.

I couldn't believe it; we were literally right across from our brother. We spent the night across from his house and we didn't even know he was in this town. Dad knocked on the door, then out of excitement, I knocked on the door. Sophie also knocked on the door, which made Dad laugh. We heard a voice from the inside approaching. The doorknob turned, and someone pulled open the door. I couldn't believe it was him. He was tall and handsome with the same scar that he had above his nose. He looked at us trying to figure out who we were.

"Geoffrey!," I exclaimed.

"My goodness what are you guys doing here," he said while he embraced Sophie and I.

"Well, we came here because of the war," I quickly answered.

"War? come in," Geoffrey said, motioning to us.

"I have to go take care of some business Geoffrey; I'm going to leave them with you. Bring them home later; I don't want their Mom coming to kill me okay?" Dad requested.

Geoffrey laughed, "okay sir," he answered.

I was surprised to hear Geoffrey call my dad sir because growing up back in Grabo I knew how much Geoffrey used to hate Dad. Perhaps they've resolved their differences and had come to a place of understanding with each other.

"You guys behave yourself okay?" dad commanded, sternly.

"Okay," I replied back.

He kissed Sophie and patted me on the head right before leaving. Geoffrey sat us down and asked us about everything. Sophie and I explained to him to the best of our knowledge about what was happening. He was amazed and perplexed by the fact that war was going on in Grabo.

"Do you know where you are right now?" he asked.

"We are in Liberia!" Sophie exclaimed.

"Yes this girl is smart," he said smiling at her.

He went over into the next room and came back with a book.

"Come over here let me show you something," he

requested while opening the book, "see, this is the map of the world, this right here is the continent of Africa."

I had seen maps before, but I've never had someone sit down and explain it to me.

"Right here is Ivory Coast where you guys came from, right next to Ivory Coast is Liberia," he explained.

He turned over to the back of the book where all the country flags were represented.

"This right here is the Liberian flag it looks similar to the United States flag," he implored.

"Why does it look similar to the United States flag?" I asked him.

"That's a good question," Geoffrey stated.

Geoffrey told Sophie and I about the long history that America and Liberia had, how the country's capital Monrovia was named after one of America's presidents James Monroe. I asked many questions, and somehow it seemed like he had all the answers. The sun was going down and I was getting hungry so I told him that he should bring us home before Mom sends JJ out to look for us. The walk back was full of more conversations about history and about America, a place that I've heard so much about but it never crossed my mind that perhaps one day America will call out to me.

I ran ahead of Geoffrey and Sophie to greet everyone and tell them about the good news.

"Where have you been?" JJ demanded, "Mom has been worried sick about you and where is Sophie?."

"Sophie is coming don't worry about it," I assured him, trying to catch my breath.

"You left your sister behind," he said sternly.

I could see that I wasn't in a good position and he was about to kick my butt. I ran outside trying to avoid confrontation and hoping to buy some time. Finally coming down the steep hill was Sophie and following behind her was Geoffrey.

"JJ!" Sophie hollered.

"You let some stranger bring Sophie home," he said to me, this time, clenching his fist.

I knew, this time, I had to spill the beans.

"No no no, it's Geoffrey!" I said out loud.

"Geoffrey?" he asked.

"Yes, Geoffrey," I said walking towards Geoffrey.

JJ walked over and embraced him. It was a family reunion like no other. Tuma came out, and she embraced him as well. She started crying and thanking God in Mom's native language. He spent a few hours with us, and we enjoyed every moment of it. Mom ended up coming home late that night because she had to work extra, so she didn't get to see him.

That night I thought about our family coming back together. I thought about school, and I thought about things going back to normal and us moving back to Ivory Coast and becoming a family again.

Chapter 12

A month had gone by, and things were still looking good. Mom and Dad were reconciling for the lost time that they had been apart. Dad was trying to make up for the bad times, to have a fresh start and a new beginning. It felt good to see Dad coming around more and to see Mom being open to talking things through. One late night Dad and Mom sat me down and told me that I was going to be starting school the following day and that I needed to stop going in the woods with the owner of the house, his son and JJ. I needed to focus on school and get good grades; that was my only job for now. I was terrified because back home after preschool we were told that we had to go to a French school. Therefore, I didn't learn much even though I had a tutor for English. It was hard for me to balance the two because the academic workload was too much. I saw in the corner of my eye a new backpack with school supplies and a uniform. I knew it was for me, and I wanted to grab it; but at the same time I didn't want Mom and Dad to think that I wanted to go to school.

That night Mom made me go to sleep earlier than everyone else. I also woke up very early the next day. Tuma had the water boiling on the fire, and the half bucket of cold water was next to the fireplace. She poured some hot water into it to keep the temperature consistent. She grabbed a brand new bar of soap and a new towel and a new scrubber. She called out to me, but this time she was gentle. She smiled at me the whole time.

"You're going to make us proud," she said, "you're going to do things for this family that nobody has ever done." It was nice hearing these words come from Tuma, yet at the same time, I knew I was just as dumb as the kid sitting next to me in class. Tuma's expectation of me was way too high for even me to reach. Instead, I smiled and pretended as if I wasn't disturbed inside by the kind words she was saying. That morning JJ walked me down a couple of blocks to where a few other kids were congregating and preparing to go to school.

"Just go to school with these kids," JJ said, in a disgruntled voice.

"Can you please come with me in case some kid tries to beat me up?" I suggested to him.

"Don't worry if any of these kids beat you up just tell me, we'll beat him up the next day," he urged.

I couldn't believe it; my own brother wanted me to get beat up. On my first day of school before beating up the kid who beats me up. I walked to where the other kids were waiting. I watched as JJ disappeared in the distance. I swallowed the saliva in my mouth and smiled at the other kids.

"My man what are you doing here," a kid on a bike said to me. I instantly became crippled by fear; I knew this was it. The first day of school I was going to get beaten up by one of these kids and JJ wasn't here to protect me. The only time I asked him to be there for me, he didn't show up. I felt betrayed, scared and out of place just like back home.

"Don't listen to him, he's just a rude kid," assured a girl with a soft voice, "everything will be alright." I felt a gentle hand on my back.

I looked up and then nodded my head up and down.

"What's your name?" she requested.

"My name is Martin," I responded back.

"What school are you going to Martin?" she questioned.

"I don't remember what the name of the school is," I responded embarrassingly.

"Oh I see I hope you find your school," she replied, then walked off.

I stood there until all the other kids were gone. I didn't know what to do. I was afraid of going back home because Tuma would beat me. I decided to just stand there until class was over then go back home when the other kids got out of class. It just so happened that there was a kid who was also heading to school late, he seemed like he was in a rush. He had on the same uniform as me.

"Hey you, my man where are you going," I asked trying to imitate Dad.

He stopped and looked at me "my man I'm going to school," the kid replied back.

"My man I'm trying to find my school man," I said sternly.

"Let's go then," he answered.

I didn't know where we were going, but it was better than standing here all alone waiting for everybody else to get out of school. After taking the same shortcut the other kids took, we passed through the woods and ended up on the other side.

"Yeah, that's the school," I said, excitingly.

"Oh my man, I go to that same school," he exclaimed.

We both walked together. As we got close, we heard the belt ring, so we both started running towards the school. All the other kids went into their classrooms. I remembered the class that Dad said I was supposed to be in. I rushed into the class and trailing right behind me was my new friend, he was also in the same class. Two seats in the back room were unoccupied. I sat in the one closer to the middle, and my new friend sat in the one closer to the corner.

"Mr. Toe, do you know what we do when you're late to class?" The teacher asked.

"I'm sorry sir it will not happen again. I didn't know where the school was," I replied.

The teacher stared at me in disbelief as if he couldn't believe what he just heard. "All right let this be the first and the last," he warned.

The teacher then addressed my new friend and told him that he was to write a three-page paper saying, 'I will not be late to school' over and over again. My new friend made a joke about the matter, and the whole class laughed. The teacher became infuriated that he wasn't taking his education seriously and told him he can leave his class if he wanted to. Again, my new friend made a joke about giving back his school fee. The teacher then threatened to talk with his parents, and that's when he finally quieted down. He was two years older than me; he had stayed back twice.

At recess, kids played tag and some would go down to the marketplace to buy food. I wanted to follow them, but I was afraid that I would be late for class again. I saw the girl that asked me which school I went to. I waved to her, but she didn't see me. 'Saint Philomena. Why couldn't I remember that?' I thought to myself.

"My man you like her go talk to her," my new friend said from behind me.

"No I don't," I added sternly, "she's my friend."

"You lie," he said arguing with me.

I felt offended, I walked away from him and went over to the other side of the school.

"My man where are you going?" he beseeched..

"Stay away from me," I said frowning back at him.

I stayed at the other corner until the bell rang. The other kids started to go back into their classes. I followed them and went back to my class hoping to avoid confrontation with my new friend. Even though I sat across from him, I avoided eye contact. I tried to listen to everything the teacher was saying and whenever he motioned to me I didn't look. The last bell went off, and everyone wrote down the homework assignment off the board. The class started to make their way out and as I was about to go to the door, the teacher called me.

"Martin," he said, "you will be staying here with your joking friend to write, 'I will not be late again'." My stomach began to growl. I should have just pretended like I didn't hear him when he called my name. All I wanted to do was go back home and eat after a long day of school. I spent two more hours writing 'I will not be late again' over and over until the teacher was satisfied. I was furious at my new friend, and I wanted to punch him in the face and tell him we were not friends. After school, I walked home, him trailing behind me. As he'd get closer, I would pick up pace. When I got home, I went straight to the kitchen, but no one was in the kitchen. I thought to myself maybe they have my food waiting inside. When I went inside, I heard a bunch of commotion and I hurried in to see what was going on. Laying down on the floor was JJ and Tuma was panicking and yelling.

My heart sank, "what is going on?" I asked.

"JJ just fell down, and he won't get up," Tuma cried out.

I went down on my knees and started yelling his name, "JJ get up!"

It seemed as if he was caught in between two worlds. He could hear me, but he couldn't snap back to reality. The lady of the house came home and saw the commotion.

"What is going?" she asked.

"JJ isn't getting up; he's just lying there," Tuma cried out.

"Everything will be okay, I need you to go get me cold water okay," the lady requested.

Tuma ran to the kitchen and grabbed cold drinking water in a bucket with a cup, the woman filled a cup and splashed it on JJ. He responded to it; she then splashed another cup on him and he responded even more.

"I think it's working!" Tuma said.

The lady then took the whole bucket and splashed it on him. He woke up as if he had a nightmare.

"What happened, who poured water on me?" he demanded.

"JJ are you okay?" Tuma questioned him.

"Was it you Martin?" he asked.

I couldn't believe it; he didn't even know what had just happened. I was going to take the blame, but the wife of the house said, "No, it was me." I thought about how I was going to explain it to him and worst, how I was going to explain it to Mom.

"Listen, Martin you can't tell Mom about this, she's already worried enough right now," Tuma questioned me. I didn't agree nor disagree to her request, knowing one way or another Mom had to find out.

That evening I told him about everything that happened. He couldn't believe a word that I said.

"What do you last remember doing?" I asked him.

"I was sitting in the chair, I decided to go get some water and then everything went black that's all," he said staring at the wall.

I felt afraid for him. What if the wife of the house

didn't show up? He could have been seriously hurt; I started to cry.

"What are you crying for?" he asked.

I wiped my tears. "Nothing," I responded.

"I will be okay alright, see," he replied flexing his muscles that he would always let me punch whenever he didn't deliver on a promise. We both walked out to the kitchen where Tuma and the wife of the house prepared a meal. JJ and I both grabbed our plates and ate, the owner of the house and his son was late coming home. This time, they didn't have the extra help from JJ. The husband advised JJ to stay home because the weather was going to be brutal.

Mom came home after a long day of work. She sat down and ate. "Did you guys hear the news?" she said.

"What news?" the owner of the house questioned.

"They say rebels are coming in town!," Mom exclaimed.

"There are no rebels, they will not make it here," the owner of the house assured.

"We will not take any chances, tomorrow we are leaving so pack your stuff," Mom said, "if anyone wants to stay, they can stay."

That night I took my books, pencils, and school materials out of my bag. I replaced them with all my new clothes. When I asked my Mom where we were going, she said, "Towards Kahnwia Camp." The next morning I saw an army truck full of soldiers patrolling the streets. That's when I knew my mother was right. I went back inside, and told her what I saw.

"You and JJ go get Geoffrey right now," she demanded.

JJ and I raced down the cracked cement sidewalk. After sprinting, we would walk for a couple of minutes then we would start running again. Along the way, we saw a young widow mourning over her dying husband. This was the first time that I've seen death in Zwedru. She begged him not to go but to stay with her. I wanted to see what was going to happen, but JJ yanked me, so we continued running. When we got to Geoffrey's house, he wasn't there; he was in the back of his house helping out. "Geoffrey we have to go, Mom said there are rebels on their way we're taking the next bus to Kahnwia Camp," I said without missing a beat. Geoffrey dropped what he was doing, he went over and told his other family members what was going on. They didn't believe him, and they told him that they were just going to go through it just like the owner of the house had said.

JJ questioned him, "are you coming or are you staying?"

"I'm coming," he said, hesitantly.

Geoffrey went inside and grabbed a small bag. He shoved a couple t-shirts and pants inside and we made our way back home. Mom grabbed her bag that was full of money. When everyone was ready, we walked down to the bus station and took the next bus into Kahnwia Camp. The bus was stopped at a barrack, the bus driver and the soldiers argued for over a half hour before taking a bribe and letting the bus through. It was hard for me to sleep on the bus because I was sitting next to a stranger who I didn't want to lay my head against. It was a rough ride, the bus kept on bouncing up and down, but we made it. We were finally, here again, the small town where the young man who once lived with us lived. We arrived at his house, this time, he greeted us and he went to get us water immediately.

"What brought you guys back here?" he inquired, after handing us a cup of water.

"They say rebels are coming to Zwedru, so we left just to be safe," Mom answered.

"Oh okay," he responded putting his head down in dismay.

"Where is Victor?" Mom requested.

"You people just missed him again, he went back to Tiehnpo," said the young man.

"Mom, can we go to Tiehnpo?" I requested.

"This would be good for the kids that way they can meet their other relatives," the young man added, "plus I have a fellow who is going there."

"Let me think about it for a moment," Mom said, turning away to think about her answer.

I went over and sat with JJ, Geoffrey, Sophie and Tuma. Mom and the young gentleman talked. After a while, she came over and said we'd be going to Tiehnpo. Sophie and I were excited to go visit Uncle Victor and meet distant relatives. Tuma, on the other hand, decided she didn't want to take another journey. She decided to stay in Kahnwia Camp and so did Geoffrey. JJ and I put our bags on our backs, Mom took some of Sophie's clothes from Tuma's bag and put it into her own bag. We waited patiently for our escort. Not long after, a tall skinny man came over with a machete in hand.

"Who are the people going to Tiehnpo?" the man with the machete inquired.

"The four of us," Mom replied.

We grabbed some water and some food for the road. We walked across the graveled road and passed in between small houses. We followed a mud trail that had been trodden many travelers. The tall forest trees protected us from the scorching sun. Along the way, my mom pointed out a different tree that had edible fruit that I got to taste. She taught us about different types of plants and what they were used for.

Along the way, we saw an orange bullet from a shotgun. Mom started to panic, but I didn't want to go back.

"If we see another one we are turning around," she said, threatening.

"It must be a hunter," the man with the machete added, "keep your eyes open."

As we were walking, I saw another orange bullet shell. Instead of pointing it out I kicked it into the woods hoping maybe Mom wouldn't see it. I succeeded in hiding it from her except for one person, JJ.

"Martin I saw what you did there," said JJ, "I'm going to tell Mom."

"Please don't tell Mom," pleading with him, "I just want to see Tiehnpo."

I could tell that he wanted me to see my tribal people as well. At the same time, he didn't want to get killed for my foolish request. He held his tongue until we came into the cocoa plantation. There we saw a group of men working on the field harvesting cocoa. A few of the men had guns near them. JJ slowly made his way back where Mom was.

"Auntie," he said to her in a whisper, "the men in the front, they have guns."

My Mom slowed down when she heard about the guns but when she saw them it was too late. We were already in the open, and the guys on the plantation had already seen her. So she pretended as if she was fixing her shoes and continued walking. They exchange hellos, and we kept on going. I knew for sure we were destined to go to Tiehnpo. Along the way we passed by a couple of villages, we crossed over a silver bridge built by some engineers. After walking for about an hour, we were finally in Tiehnpo.

"This is the town," the man declared.

We walked in the middle of the village and made our way to Victor's house where we were greeted and welcomed by Victor and some of the people of the village. That night the village people prepared lots of food, we ate until we were content. That same evening, the village people danced around the fire, played music and told stories. I wanted to go outside to watch them, but Uncle Victor would not let me. The only way I could get close was by asking Uncle Victor to take me out to the bathroom to pee. That night he took me out, I could feel the heat from the campfire that illuminated the night. I heard men and women cheering and shouting, the sound of drums and other instruments playing melodies. I wanted to go closer and see, but Uncle Victor did not want me to. The next day I woke up with a bloated stomach. I tried to move around but I couldn't, I went to my Mom and told her what was happening.

"Your sister doesn't feel well too," she said in a concerned tone.

JJ seemed to be fine and Mom seemed to be fine as well, it was just Sophie and I. JJ took me to the kitchen and he told me to rub some ashes on my stomach. I thought it was funny so I did it anyways even though I knew I had to take a shower afterward. I went into Victor's room; I slept on my stomach. Then I started releasing gas, after a couple of hours I felt great. Sophie on the other hand, was still feeling sick.

The kids in the village wanted to play with me; I asked my Mom if I could play with them. She told me yes on the condition that I refuse any offer of food. We ran off to play a game of tag and hide and seek. Later on, we went down to where the water place was. The water used for washing clothes providing water for animals. The stream wasn't too wide nor too steep, but it was a good size one. The other kids knew how to swim and they asked me to join them, but I said no because I didn't know how to swim. Some of them thought I was just scared of getting into the water, so they made it their objective to get me into the water one way or another. I tried to run away but one of them was faster than me, he tackled me to the ground and the others grabbed my legs, picking me up and carrying me to the water. They then pushed me into the water and luckily, JJ came out of nowhere and grabbed me out of the water. He pushed me away from the other kids, and they all ran away. I started to cry; he didn't ask me why I was crying. He looked at me as if annoyed at how I was handling business.

"You need to be strong," he said staring sternly at my face, "don't let those kids do that to you." We walked back home; Sophie was still sick and it looked like she had gotten progressively worst. Mom was scared for her; she didn't want anything to happen to her. I went inside, grabbed a towel and a fresh pair of clothes out of my bag. I then went to the kitchen to boil some hot water to take a bath.

That night we went to sleep early, there was no music, there was no celebration. The town was silent and it started to rain hard the next morning. Everyone stayed inside and watched as the rain fell down onto the dry ground. Uncle Victor and I sat on his porch and watched the empty village. It was the perfect time to ask questions about the Toe family. He told me the history of the Toe family and he pointed out some of my uncles and cousins who were walking by. I was surprised some of the people that he pointed out looked just like dad. He told me about the Williams and how they were also part of the Toe family except they had different last names. He told me about my grandfather and my grandmother and how they had passed away a few years before we came to visit. It was everything that I wanted to hear about my lineage, but I was sad that my grandparents passed away.

That day I asked Mom how Sophie was doing. "She'll get better" she sighed.

"Where is she?" I inquired.

"She's inside sleeping."

I went inside to see her, I looked at her and kissed her on the forehead, just like Dad did back in Zwedru.

"Get better for me okay?" I requested, then walked out.

I hugged my Mom and told her that she would be all right. JJ sat on the porch with his thumb in his mouth looking into the distance. I went over and sat right next to him hoping to catch a glance at what he was looking at. We spent the whole day on the porch watching the rainfall. The little kids seized the opportunity and ran out to play in the puddle. The rain later calmed down and gave us enough time to eat dinner and shower.

Another day gone, we went to sleep. The next morning Mom didn't wake up early like she usually did. JJ slept in since Mom wasn't up. Uncle Victor was up, and I heard him and another man bickering outside the bedroom door. When I went outside, I saw a table on the porch and on the table was a scale. The man had something in a small plastic bag. Uncle Victor took the bag and poured it out onto the scale. He and the man started talking as if they were negotiating a deal. I came outside to see what was going on.

"Uncle Victor what is that? I asked, curious to know.

"That's gold," he responded, "I'm trying to buy it from this young man, he got it from a riverside not too far away from here."

I looked at the object, it was shining and enticing. I've

seen gold chains before but I've never seen it in its pure elemental form. The man and Uncle Victor talked until they came to a place of agreement. I went into the room Mom, Sophie and JJ were staying in to check up on them. Mom and JJ were still sleeping; Sophie was laying in the bed staring at me. I wanted to tell Mom to wake up and that Sophie was doing better but when she saw me, she closed her eyes and pretended as if she was sleeping. I knew I couldn't make a joke to get her up because I would get in trouble.

The village people were nice and they lived a simple lifestyle. They were all close and enjoyed each other's company. They understood what was important; they understood that greed was destructive. So they shared what they harvested with the whole village, everyone was fed and clothed.

Mom and JJ had missed breakfast that morning. The noon sun was rising up high in the sky. Uncle Victor brought lunch for Mom, Sophie, and JJ but Mom refused to eat unless Sophie ate. I didn't know why she chooses to do that, but it made me angry. I thought about ways to convince Sophie to eat, but she won't eat. Mom was getting frustrated with me giving Sophie trouble and told me to go play with my friends. One of the things Sophie enjoyed was when I let her ride on my back when we played. While Mom and JJ were outside on the porch, I sneaked into their room where Sophie was sleeping.

"Hey Sophie I know you're not sleeping," I said in a soft voice, "I'll let you ride on my back if you wake up and eat and when we get back I'll buy you Kool-Aid but if you don't, I will never let you ride on my back."

I saw her little hands stretch out and touch my face. Her hands were warm hotter than the heat that I felt from the bonfire the other night. I rested my head against her hand for a moment, hoping to absorb some of the heat from her. I walked out afterward and went to go play with the other kids. It was almost night time when I came back. I was afraid my mom would beat my butt for being out too late. Instead, when I got home they were all rejoicing, my mother was smiling.

"Martin, your sister, is doing better," Mom proclaimed, smiling.

Sophie dug her head into my Mom's stomach hoping to hide. I was happy that Sophie was feeling better, it meant that Mom was going to eat and not get sick. Tiehnpo was great, I enjoyed it, but it came with a lot of worries and new problems. After spending three weeks, Mom decided it was time for us to make our journey back to the town. The village kids didn't want me to go; they wanted me to stay so they came up with a plan to hide me until my Mom left. However, I told them I needed to go with my Mom and be there with my sister. The journey back was shorter; we took a different way back home. When we got back to Kahnwia, I had a better appreciation for the town. The village life was taught, and it wasn't the type of life I saw myself living. We thanked the man who brought us back. Mom paid him some money; then we went our separate ways.

We went to the house where the young man who

once lived with my Mom lived. When we entered the house, we saw Geoffrey sitting down eating and having a conversation with the young men.

"We're back!," I exclaimed out loud.

The young man didn't seem too happy to see us back so early. Even though it had been a while since he'd last seen us.

"Hi auntie," he said, this time making eye contact, "how was the trip?"

"The trip was good, the kids had fun, where is Tuma?" Mom requested, abruptly.

"Tuma went to the marketplace to get some stuff, she will be back soon," he explained while trying to avoid eye contact, "would you like anything to drink?" he added.

"No thank you," Mom responded, "do you know when the next bus is going back to Zwedru?"

"Auntie the next bus should be going soon," he said to Mom.

"Alright everyone pack your things and head down to the bus stop," Mom commanded.

We were all packed up and ready to head back. Tuma walked in unexpectedly and discovered that we had returned. "Oh Auntie I didn't know you came back," Tuma said surprisingly.

"We just came back recently, we're getting the stuff ready and we're going back to Zwedru," Mom explained, "the rebels left."

Tuma had a bag of groceries in her hand and a guilty look on her face. A newer bus with fewer passengers came to the bus stop and we loaded our luggage. Mom and

Sophie shared a seat, JJ and Geoffrey both shared a seat, and Tuma and I shared a seat. The whole ride neither Mom nor Tuma exchanged words; I knew something was wrong but I didn't know what it was. When we got to the barrack, the soldiers refused to let us into Zwedru. They checked the entire bus; they also made every adult get off.

I remembered one of the soldiers who stopped us while we were going to Tiehnpo. I heard one of the soldiers say his name, he came and got on the bus. He looked around and searched high and low. Right when he was about to leave I said his name he looked back and asked,"who said my name?" the soldier replied.

All of the other kids looked at me. I smiled at him and as he approached me.

"How do you know my name," he asked with a curious look on his face.

"I remember you," I responded back.

He smiled at me and walked away, "alright bus is good to go," he yelled out.

Every adult climbed back on the bus, and we were free to go. I waved goodbye to him through the window; he waved back.

"Sit down," the bus driver instructed.

"How do you know that soldier?" JJ inquired.

It seemed like my whole family plus everybody else on the bus was interested and wanted to know. They all stared at me waiting to hear my answer. "I just remember him from the last time we passed to go to Tiehnpo," I said in a soft voice.

"So you don't know him?" JJ said out loud, then sat

back in his seat as if the conversation was over. We got back to Zwedru; nothing had changed. We went back to the house where we were staying. It was evening; the sun was setting and it was getting dark. The wife of the house and Tuma made dinner. Still, Mom and Tuma were not talking. Usually when they did this, it only lasted for one day. I figured by tomorrow they would have put aside their differences and become friends again. What would happen next was nothing any of us were prepared for.

Chapter 13

The next morning everything was the same, JJ woke up earlier than me and took a bath just like he usually did before I had a chance to. Mom went out to do business in the marketplace. Tuma was cooking, and Geoffrey was back at his house preparing to go to school. I saw that JJ was behaving a little funny, but it wasn't something out of his norm as he was a jokester by nature. Tuma boiled the hot water which she usually did and bathed me. I went into the room we were staying in and put on a fresh pair of clothes. I decided to go join JJ in the living room to talk when I saw him clenching his stomach. He looked at me as if in despair, I didn't know what to make of it. I didn't know if he was playing around or if it was serious. I watched as he collapsed to the ground. I ran out to get Tuma; she ran in, but at that point, he was struggling to gasp for air. She screamed his name, but he didn't respond she started to cry and bellow, "Please come back." The wife of the house came and asked what going on, I then told her that it had happened again. This time, JJ isn't responding at all. A strong smell came from him. He threw up all the food he had eaten, and his body turned cold.

"Go get your mother," the lady instructed me.

I started running. I didn't look back, but instead of going to find Mom, I ran to where Dad worked, he was talking with someone at his work.

"Dad I need to speak to you right now," I interrupted.

"Give me a minute," he said.

"JJ just passed away," I interjected.

He and the stranger he was talking to both sighed in grief.

"Let me shut this down, I'll be right on my way," he said.

I ran back home as fast as I could, when I got home they were cleaning him up. Tuma was crying, and she didn't want to go close to the body, so the lady cleaned him up and then put his new clothes on him, the ones he never got to wear. Not long afterward, dad arrived on the scene with that same gentleman in the truck; they came with a couple of blankets to wrap his body before preparing his body for a proper burial. Before they were able to take his body Mom came home. She wept bitterly; Tuma was crying, the wife of the house cried. Sophie cried because Mom was crying and I was heartbroken. The house was filled with mourning. That night I tried to fall asleep but fear gripped me. I couldn't sleep, no matter how hard I tried I was afraid that death would soon get to catch me. It was daybreak, the sun came out, and that was when I felt like it was safe enough to go to sleep. I slept until noon, the next day Geoffrey came over to visit. He had no idea what had recently happened when Mom told him, he broke down and started crying. I felt my heart break all over again; the pain was unbearable and I didn't know how to deal with it. I tried to be strong but inside I was broken and felt a void that only JJ filled. That evening the wife of the house cooked, Geoffrey and I shared a dish. This time, I decided not to eat, I tried but nothing tasted good, everything was bitter in my mouth. Geoffrey started to cry again, and my heart broke even more.

"Martin why isn't you crying," he asked, with tears running down his cheeks.

"I try, but the tears just won't come out," I said looking at him, "I don't know how to cry anymore."

He looked at me and said, "everything will be alright, eat."

I tried, but I couldn't do that either. I left the area where we were eating and went to go sit in the dining room by myself. Sophie poked her head in and asked if I was alright. I wanted to tell her to leave me alone, but I couldn't even say that. She watched me as I struggled to come back to this reality but was trapped in another one. The next few days, things were not the same. Mom went to work, but came home earlier than she usually did.

Months had passed by; it seemed like everyone was doing better. It felt as if they had all forgotten JJ. They were moving on, but I was stuck, I didn't know where he was, I didn't know if he was safe, all I knew was that he wasn't coming back.

I overheard Mom and Dad talking about me going back to school. I didn't feel like I was ready. I didn't want to go back to school. Whenever I tried to argue with my mom, she would always tell me I didn't have my own will. Whenever she said that, that meant I was going whether I liked it or not. The next day dad and I went shopping for school supplies, Mom went to the market place but came home early. While she was in the marketplace making business, Tuma went into her room and grabbed most of her money, packed her bag and left. While she was leaving, the wife of the house asked her where she was going but she didn't say a thing to her, and that was the last time we've heard from Tuma.

Chapter 14

"Martin wakes up," a gentle voice echoed in my ear. "Leave me alone," I groaned arguing back while rolling on the other side of the bed.

I opened one eye to peek and see what was happening. I watched as Sophie walk back to where Mom was standing. Mom reached on the small dresser for the little bottle of powder, grabbed it and put some around Sophie's neck. She grabbed a fresh pair of clothes out of her bag to put on Sophie. Mom then looked at me and I quickly closed my eyes hoping she thought that I was still sleeping.

"Martin won't get up," Sophie complained.

"Go to the kitchen and get some food," Mom instructed her, "I'll be right there."

"Martin get up you have school today," Mom said in a loud voice.

I groaned again hoping she would leave me alone.

"All your friends are going to school, now get up and get ready to go to school," she said persistently.

"I don't feel good," I said hoping perhaps that would sway her.

"I'll give you some Ibuprofen," she said, that was her first time to go for a drug for any symptom.

"When you get back from school I'll make sure Augustine comes to get you," she added.

Spending the day with my dad was more than enough to make me happy. I rolled out of bed and got my flip flops on. I went into the kitchen where the hot water was boiling. My mother dumped some hot water into a half full bucket of cold water. Sophie sat in the kitchen and ate her breakfast. Mom grabbed the bucket full of water, sponge and a bar of soap. She bathed me and as she did she began to weep, it broke my heart. After bathing me, she wiped me down. Then she put some powder around my neck and under my arm, she dressed me up in my new school uniform that Dad had bought for me. She put my socks on me and helped me lace up my Timberland boots. The wife of the house had already prepared a bowl for me; Sophie was done eating. I took my time and ate the food.

"You only have a few minutes," Mom added, "you don't want to be late."

I took my last few bites, went back inside and grabbed my backpack.

"Do you want me to walk you guys to school," Mom asked.

"No, I know where to go," I said to her.

I grabbed Sophie's hand and rushed up the little hill.

"Be careful with your sister," my mom said from behind.

I didn't want us to be late, so I asked her to jog with me. At times she would get tired and slow down, but then I would convince her that we were racing so she would pick up speed and I would let her win. We got to the place where all the other kids congregated before going to school. Instead of waiting for them, I told her we should get a leading start before they catch up to us. So Sophie and I walked through the woods by ourselves to get to school. When we got to school, there were only a few kids on campus. It was an early morning; the sky was cloudy and the morning dew covered the ground. She and I stood outside and watched as the other kids made their way to the campus. The courtyard was packed, and everybody was excited to be back in school. Everyone was smiling and enjoying their friends' company. Sophie saw her schoolmates and decided to go join them. I watched as she disappeared into the crowd, anxiously waiting for the school bell to ring so that we could all go into our classes.

Then it happened, the first gunshot went off. I saw the smoke from the residue of the shot. The younger kids started to panic; then the second shot went off. After that the third, the fourth, by this time everyone was running for their life. I glance into the crowd but I couldn't find Sophie, fear gripped me. I figured she had already started running back with the other kids. I started running back home hoping to find her.

Along the way, I asked others, "have you seen small girl name Sophie?"

None of them knew who she was. I was scared of going back on campus, but I knew I couldn't go back home without Sophie. I started to race back to the old plantation. Then I accidentally bumped into someone; it was my old friend, the one who got me into trouble.

"My man, have you seen my sister?" I said to him.

"My man, your sister, is back there." he said pointing at the campus.

"Thank you!," I exclaimed.

I continued racing back to the school. As I was leaving the plantation, I saw a young girl frantic and panting. My heart calmed down in the midst of chaos.

"Oh, Sophie are you okay!," I inquired while hugging her.

"Yes," she replied, nodding her head up and down.

"We have to go find Mom," I explained to her.

We started running through the old plantation field. We caught up to some of the people that I asked if they had seen my sister. They asked me if that was the little girl I was looking for, and I told them yes. The shots were still firing. Sophie and I raced home, when we got there the whole place was vacated. I checked the house but no one was home, I saw that Mom had left her bag full of money behind. The bathroom had steam, as if someone was still showering. Sophie and I put down our backpacks in the house. We followed the crowd of people running away hoping maybe we'd find our mother along the way. The people started splitting up going two ways. Others were taking the road towards Kahnwia Camp, and others took the road towards the Konobo District.

When Sophie and I got to that junction, immediately, she wanted to go towards the road she was more familiar with. Which was the one we took while coming into

Liberia as well as when we ran away because of the rumors of war. Something didn't seem right to me, for some reason I didn't want to go that way.

"No Sophie," I responded, "we can't go that way." She began to cry, but I had my reasons. I told her that Mom and the others were waiting for us in the Konobo area. Hoping maybe that would make her stop crying and it did for a little bit. I told her everything was going to be alright; we were going to find Mom. I was familiar with the road we were on; it was the same one the owner of the house, his son, JJ and I took when we went to the farm. This time, the small path that led into the forest that took us to the owner's farm was now cramped with a bunch of people running for their life. There was one man in particular who had a shotgun in his hand. He seemed frantic and didn't know what to do so he stashed the shotgun into the woods. I looked around and saw no one else wanted to pick it up, so I picked it up. Even though I didn't know how to use it. I felt like I could use it to protect Sophie from the rebels.

"What are you doing?" a stranger said from behind me.

"I need to protect my sister and me," I answered.

"You better put down that gun before they kill you," the stranger argued.

The fellow who owned gun saw that I was carrying it he came back and look at me sternly and said, "young man put down the gun and run for your life."

I instantly dropped the gun; fear gripped me. I grabbed Sophie's hand and started running. We came out of the forest into an open road. I felt happy and thought perhaps this was where the journey came to an end, but I was wrong. I saw no one going down the open road, everyone crossed the road and continued through the forest. We started hearing bombs and heavy artilleries, others started running even faster.

"They're getting close," someone said, panicked.

I thought about the Mom, I thought about Dad, and I thought about Sophie. Tears came to my eyes, and I started crying, I tried to be brave, but I was afraid. I was afraid of never getting to see Mom again. I was worried that something bad might have happened to Dad. Sophie looked at me, and I tried to hide my tears, but it was too much to hide.

"Young man, don't cry everything will be alright," another stranger said.

I nodded my head up and down, and we continued walking and running. When the firing slowed down, we started walking again. A group of people passed before us and amongst them was a lady that Sophie and I were introduced to by our dad.

"Martin that's the lady," Sophie declared excitingly.

"What lady?" I urged, frustrated.

"The one that's friends with dad," Sophie responded back, "she might know where Mom and Dad are."

"Let's walk for a little bit, and then we'll try to see if it's her," I said back to Sophie.

"It's her, it's her, it's her," she argued back.

"Alright Sophie you need to stop," I said looking her in the face, "let's wait until we get on the open road so we can check and see okay?"

She looked at me mad and frustrated, but I knew it just wasn't the right time. We stared at the lady and her friends until we came out to the open road. Sophie let go of my hand and ran towards the woman.

"Sophie!" I called out but she was already sprinting away.

She embraced the lady and the lady almost fell down. The woman was afraid for her life, and Sophie almost gave her a heart attack.

"What is this?" the lady questioned.

Sophie looked up at her and smiled.

"Whose child is this?" she requested looking around.

I made my way up to apologize for my sister's rude behavior. Then I realized it was her.

"Hi auntie my name is Martin Toe, I am Augustine Toe's son."

"Augustine Toe!" she exclaimed, "Where is your father?"

"Auntie, where don't know where our father or mother are. My sister and I were in school when people started shooting; we are trying to find our Mom."

"Oh ya," she exclaimed, nodding her head up and down.

"Are you guys with anyone right now?" she questioned.

"No auntie," I responded back.

"Don't worry ya," she reassured confidently, "we'll find your parents."

We walked to the next town. We went around asking people if they had seen my mother. Everyone we talked to said no, they had not seen her. That night the people who lived in the house that we stayed at fed us. A gentleman with a motorcycle came into the house that we were staying in. He was only staying for a little while, and he wanted someone to watch his motorcycle.

"Hey young man can you watch my motorcycle I'll give you something before I leave," he asked me.

"Okay sir" I responded.

I sat on the back porch of the house imagining seeing Mom again. I imagined everything going back to normal. I felt numb and lonely, the world that I knew wasn't the same. I wanted to blame God for taking JJ away, but I didn't know who He was. I didn't have a reason to care about life anymore. I didn't care if someone killed me. I was tired of running, and I was ready to give up. The gentleman came out and thanked me for watching his bike; he gave me a dollar patted me on the head got on his bike and drove off. I went inside and told the auntie what had happened. Then I handed her the dollar. She promised that she would keep it for me.

Early the next morning, I woke to go around telling people that Linda Tarwo's kids are looking for her. It seemed like nobody knew her, not like they did back in Grabo. I spent the whole day sitting on the porch hoping maybe she had heard the news. Night came and they called me in to eat, but I still didn't want to leave the porch. After eating, I ran back outside hoping maybe she didn't pass by. The next day came it was the same thing, another day passed still no news of my mom. By this time I had lost all hope. A few days had gone by and I stopped asking people about her. I was lonely, traumatized and depressed. I felt like this was it, Sophie and I were not going to be able to see our mom ever again. Sophie poked her little head out the door and made her way to where I was sitting.

"Is Mom coming?" she asked.

"No Sophie I don't think Mom is ever coming," I replied despairingly.

She frowned at me, "no Mom is coming," she yelled then ran back in the house to the auntie. I wanted to believe her so badly, but this looked hopeless after a few days of not hearing any news from Mom. I knew it would have to take a miracle. That day I went inside much earlier than I usually did. I ate with the other kids, and I went to sleep earlier than usual. Early the next morning we heard a motorcycle. The man stopped at the house and parked his motorcycle in front of the house. He knocked on the door, one of the ladies that lived in the house opened the door. I heard them talking.

"No not here," the lady said then she closed the door.

I opened the door and ran after the man, "Sir what are you looking for," I asked.

He looked at me and started up his motorcycle.

"You wouldn't happen to see some missing kids around here," he asked not expecting an answer.

I felt a chill come over my body and at that moment I wondered if he was looking for us.

With no hesitation, I said, "yes sir, my sister and I are trying to find our mom, her name is Linda Tarwo."

"What's her name again?" he asked, curiously.

"Linda Tarwo," I said in a louder voice.

His eyes lit up as if he was surprised to hear that name.

"Alright stay right here," he said.

"Okay," I answered back.

Then he drove off down the road and disappeared over the hill. For a moment I thought we were finally going to see our Mom but that hope just drove away. I went back inside feeling sad and downcasted. I went back and lay down on the mat that I was sleeping on. The lady that had opened the door came to me and asked me what we were talking about. I explained to her that he was looking for some missing kids. I told her that Sophie and I were looking for our mother.

"Oh man!" she exclaimed, "why didn't you tell me this, I told the man that there were no missing kids here, only my sister's kids." She felt guilt and wanted to make up for the mistake that she had done. She asked me to go get my sister; she would bring us over to the next town to go search for my mother. So I went over into the next room where Sophie was sleeping next to our auntie and woke her up. We both washed our face and got ready to go over to the next town. As we were leaving, we heard a motorcycle coming. We looked around, but we couldn't see it. The motorcycle started getting closer and closer. Then out of the valley, it came out. It was the same one that we saw earlier but this time there was a passenger on the backside. He was heading to the house we were leaving. I couldn't believe it. The passenger in the back seat was a short woman holding on for her dear life.

"Sophie that's Mom!," I exclaimed out loud.

Without knowing where Mom was, Sophie started yelling.

"Mom, Mom, Mom." I joined her, and soon enough the motorcyclist heard us, and he drove our direction. She got off the motorcycle and embraced us. She held onto us, and she didn't want to let us go. The more she squeezed, the more life comes back into my lonely heart. She thanked the motorcyclist for finding us. He put on his helmet, told us to take care, then he drove off. She then thanked the lady who was bringing us to the next town. I felt energized and ready for the journey.

We talked and walked all day until we got to a small village where we spent the night. The people of the village fed us and took care of us. The next day we traveled some more, on the way we met a gentleman from Liberia whom my Mom knew growing up. This gentleman traveled with us and showed us the way to get to the border and get back into Ivory Coast.

Before getting to the border, we stopped in a small village where there was no more than ten people living there, they lived off the land and harvested yam. That night we had yam for dinner. One of the kids that lived in the village was my age. He and I went to the woods to play; he told me how he was the next chief of the village. I asked him, "How do you become chief?"

"Your family has to either marry into the chief family or you have to kill the chief," he said with a straight face. At that moment I knew one thing for sure. I did not want to be chief because I didn't want anyone trying to kill me. He and I had a great conversation and then later on, we went back to the village. For some reason, my mother didn't want to stay in that small village. So in the middle of the night she woke us up, and we started walking to the next village. When we got to the next village, we saw people packing their stuff and heading to the other village. My Mom carried Sophie on her back, I wanted to sleep, but my Mom didn't want us to stop. We followed the group of people journeying to the next village. They were carrying all different sorts of thing from meat to fur, gold, diamond and more. They made their living off trading, and they were on their regular route to go to Ivory Coast.

When we got to the next village, we stopped at a small house. The man living there offered us the last bit of food and water that he had, but my Mom refused it. She asked him how long the journey would be. He told us the borders was not too long from there. We were less than twenty minutes. I rested my head against the wood that held the roof of the house to catch some sleep as my Mom and the man talked. Not long afterward, everything was silent.

"Martin let's go, we don't want to miss the boat crossing," Mom said in a hurry. I jumped up from my sleep and went outside, waiting for Mom and Sophie to get ready. We followed behind the other merchants. When we got to the river, the land was higher than the river. We had to climb down some rocks where the others were waiting for the man who went back and forth taking people across the river on a raft. When it was our turn we got on the raft and the man paddled left and right. The water was brown just like the Cavalla River. There were huge whirlpools in the water. I stuck my hand in the water to feel it, but my Mom was once again petrified.

"Martin you better take your hand out of that water," she commanded. I took my hand out of the water to not terrify her. When we got to the other side, a man grabbed a rope and tossed it to the man on the raft. The other man pulled the raft onto land. We slowly got off the raft trying not to fall into the water. We then climbed up the hill onto flat land. We sat down with the other travelers waiting for others to make their way across then we started walking again. We walked for a little while but because of the company of others it didn't feel that long. The small path led to an open road; there we saw a truck that was parked around the truck with other people who also brought things to trade. They brought clothing, bread, butter and other kinds of things. We watched as the people did business with each other at noon time everyone was done. The people from the town got on the truck. Mom, Sophie and I got on the truck with them, and we made our way back in town. The people in the truck seemed happy and excited. I thought to myself, do these people know what's going on in the world? I was perplexed and confused that people could be happy when others are suffering in the world and trying to run away for their life. When we got in town everybody got off to head to their homes. Sophie, Mom and I got off the truck and watched as everyone walked away. We stood by the truck with nowhere to go. A short lady approached us; she saw us standing by the truck.

"What are you doing here standing by the car?" she asked us.

"It's our first time coming here we don't know anyone here," Mom replied back.

The woman quickly replied, "come on let's go to my house, what are you doing standing here."

We followed her, passing in between houses made of both bricks and mud. We went past a pharmacy and some abandoned houses. Then we came to a three room house, one was occupied by her son, the other one was occupied by her husband's brother, and the third room was occupied by her and her husband. The lady's name was Fleuron Garleh; they had an animal farm where they raised chicken, guinea pigs and other types of animals. That evening the family fed us and gave us a place to sleep.

The next day Mom started finding ways to start making business. She started making food and going along with the other people who traded stuff to sell. She would leave with a huge tube of food and come back with an empty tube. After a few weeks of staying with Fleuron and her family, we were able to get our own place. Mom didn't want me to stay home and get in trouble with the town boys, so she sent me to be an apprentice for a tailor just like she did back in Grabo. Each morning I would wake up extra early to help Mom out by carrying her stuff to the place where the merchants would meet. Then afterward I would go back home and sleep. When it got lighter out I would take Sophie over to the neighbor's house, then I would make my way back home then get ready to go help out at the tailor's shop. At noon time I would go to the marketplace and buy my favorite food, achecīr. I realized that in Liberia they didn't have achecīr, a Liberian woman in the market place told me and I was greatly disappointed. In the evening I would come back home to find Mom and Sophie already there waiting for me. Mom would cook us a meal, and we would get ready to go to sleep afterwards. This became our regular routine for a few months. Mom was becoming well known in the community, and she was well respected.

There was rumors and news circulating that there were different countries receiving refugees into their land because of the war in Liberia and Ivory Coast. My mother investigated into the matter and found out that it was true. The following week my mother didn't wake up early and cook like she normally did to sell to the traders. Instead, she slept in and didn't go to sell food at the trading place. We woke up early, packed our belongings and took a bus to Guiglo. It was about an hour drive. When we got to the barrack, the car was stopped, and every adult was checked before entering the city. The streets were noisy, and the people were going back and forth. It was nice to be in the city again. When we got off the bus, we took a cab into a small town called Peace Town, which was a fifteen-minute drive outside the city to register.

One of Mom's old friends who she had helped back in the day was there; his name was Dale Jacque. He was able to look through the system and find all our paperwork and made it easier for us. After we had registered, we got on another taxi back into the city. From there we took another bus back to Zagne. On our way to Zagne, there was a car accident. Traffic was stopped going both ways; everyone got off the busses. A crowd swarmed around as if it was a group of vultures near a carcass. I made my way to see what was going on while still staying close to Mom. I couldn't believe it; a young man laid motionless on the floor. Everyone else had survived the crash except for him.

"What is it?" Mom asked me.

"It's a young man; he's dead," I whispered to her hoping Sophie wouldn't hear me.

She grabbed my hand and grabbed Sophie's and marched us back to the bus. After a while everyone else got on the bus, the driver started up the engine. He honked a few times then drove up the hill. He picked up speed and off we went. We got back to Zagne late at night. Mom woke up early in the morning to cook and go with the others for the trade. That morning instead of waking me up like she usually did, she let me sleep in and went by herself. The next morning I brought Sophie to the next door neighbors. Instead of going to the tailor shop I went out to play with my friends. I did this until one day the tailor caught me and asked me where I've been the past few weeks. I was afraid that he would tell my Mom, so I ran off without giving him an explanation. Two days later he showed up at my house. He had a conversation with my mom about my absence. After he left my mom sat me down and asked me why I haven't been showing up. I told her that I wasn't being treated fairly at the shop. She and I came to an agreement. If I wasn't being treated fairly, I didn't have to go anymore.

When I went back to the shop, the tailor treated me

with care and respect. I started feeling more at home and continued going there more often. A month and a half had gone by, and we did not hear anything about the results. The following week we heard the news that my Mom's name was on the bulletin. That same day we made a trip back to Guiglo and took a cab to Peace Town. Upon our arrival into Peace Town, gunshots started going off and people started running for their lives. We got back in the cab and told the driver to bring us back to the city. It had been so long since I'd last heard gunshots. The people running brought back memories of the very thing we were trying to get away from.

We drove back to town Mom told the driver to bring us to the closest hotel. We spent the night in a one bedroom hotel next to a bar. The music was playing all night long until the last person left. It felt good to sleep on a mattress again and to have a pillow to rest my head against. We slept great, and the next morning we woke up early and took a cab back into Peace Town. When we got into town, people were lined up to see if their names were on the bulletin. We got in line with the rest of the others, and sure enough, Mom's name was on the bulletin. After grabbing our package, we got on the bus that was going to bring us to our next destination Abidjan. When we lived in Grabo Mom would send us to Abidjan to go to school and to live with some of her friends. I was familiar with the place we were going, and I was excited about the journey.

There were lots of buses all packed filled with people. Sophie, Mom and I were seated together. I had the window seat that way I could watch everything that was going on. When we came to Yamoussoukro, the bus driver stopped, and the people got off the bus for some fresh air. They gave us food and water. After the intermission we got back on the bus and drove for a few hours, we finally made it to Abidjan. The bus that we were in came to a stop at a large building that was enclosed by a very large brick fence. We all got off the bus one by one, and we were each given a ticket before heading out of the bus. This was our ticket to get in the gates. It was a night out, and the clouds covered the sky. The only thing that was visible was the moonlight from inside the four walls of the gate. People scrambled around to find a place to sleep. Each person was assigned a room to share with another. We were all given small mattresses to lay on and share with family members. Others put their mattresses together and made a much larger mattress. Some people were given the rooms upstairs, and others were given rooms downstairs. Others preferred sleeping in the hallway instead of sharing a room with strangers.

The next morning I woke up early to get a good look at the new compound that we were staying in. There was a big sandbox to play in the backyard. Right next to it was an outside kitchen as well as a table to sit on. We were all given a portion of food for the week; each room was assigned a gas stove with instructions. On the first day, people struggled to figure out how it worked. When hunger struck they all put their minds together and finally figured it out. The compound was always noisy; people were always bickering and fighting. There was a lot of stealing taking place. Yet, somehow on Sunday, they would all manage to put aside their differences to worship together.

I started making some friends in the new compound. We entertained ourselves by playing chess, tag and telling stories. As time went along, the adults were given the freedom to go out of the gate as long as they returned back at a certain time. Some nights there would be gunfires, other nights there would be helicopters trolling the sky. We all lived in constant fear of being ambushed or set up by the Ivorian Government because of the way they behaved in Peace Town.

A couple of weeks later we got on the bus again and went for the interview. We were asked about ourselves, our story and why we wanted to go to their country. That day we also went through the fingerprint process as well as the identification process. After doing all the paperwork, the buses brought us back to the compound. Everyone was excited, others told their story to others, and they were praised. There was one man, in particular, his name is Vinny. Vinny was nothing like any of the other residents. He had flashy ways of talking and an odd way of pronouncing things. One gentleman asked Vinny what he had told the interviewers.

"Well," he said as he cleared his throat.

"I told them during the war, I was put in prison, but I got out of jail, grabbed the gun and escaped. I ran for my own safety."

Another fellow asked, "what did you say when they asked you why you should go to America?"

"Well, I'm very educated, and I'm more qualified to go to America than anybody here," he said confidently. Everyone started to laugh and thought he was playing.

"There is nothing funny," he replied, with a serious face.

"My man if Vinny passes the test then we all going to America," another person said from the crowd.

The crowd erupted in laughter; some walked away telling the story to others. Others asked him more questions to see what else he would say.

There were a few guys who lived in the compound who knew how to cut hair. So all the men would gravitate to them. Sophie found new friends and would run around with them, but Mom would always tell me to keep an eye out for her.

One afternoon after a hot day, the moon was out. The sky was calm, and everything was going well. Then I heard a commotion; people were yelling and screaming. I followed the crowd of people to see what was going on. When I got there, I saw a young guy who I played checkers with a few days ago who got mad at me because I kept on beating him. He was laying on the ground having a seizure. People stood and watched as he suffered, I felt like it was happening again. Then out of nowhere a man came from the crowd and wrapped himself around the kid on the floor.

"Why are you guys standing around watching the poor boy suffer," the guy holding the kid down said in a loud voice. Everyone was feeling ashamed, and they all walked away one by one until there was no one left. Then the boy's parents came, but by then he had already come out of the seizure. Ever since then he kept to himself and he never talked to anyone. Some time had passed, and a lot of the people had forgotten why they were in the compound, but soon they found out.

Chapter 15

One early morning, an unexpected box was delivered to the doorkeeper. He was given specific instructions on what to do. The men that were looked up to and regarded as leaders were called over and told to get the people ready. Yet, they were not to tell the people why they needed to get ready. Somehow rumors started going around that the results were in without even looking in the box. Everyone rushed outside, people were trying to get their hands on the box. The Doorkeeper threatened to send the box back if the people didn't conduct themselves. Finally, they got a control of the situation. The people were lined up one by one and were each called and given their letter. Some of them could not read so others read the letter for them. When some open their letter, they saw that they had passed the interview processes and were heading to either Europe, America, Canada or so forth. Others open their letters, and they found out the harsh truth that they were not going anywhere. There was rejoicing, and there was crying. Some people lived in the same room as we did that didn't make it. There was another person that did. Vinny got his letter, and everybody crowded around him to see what his results was. When he opened up he glanced at the opening words 'Vinny; we thank you for going through our interview process, but you did not qualify ...,' when he found out that he wasn't going, he justified not being picked to go because of the government.

Then my mother's name was called, the others made way for her. She slowly made her way up, grabbed her envelope and ran back into the room. Sophie and I followed after her.

"Open the envelope sister Linda," a lady watching from the outside said.

"Yes open it, Mom," I said anxiously.

She was afraid to open it. She handed it to another lady and asked her to open it. Then Mom turned away and started walking out of the room because she was afraid the results would be bad. The lady opened the envelope pulled out the letter. She unfolded it and started to read from the top, 'Linda, we thank you for going through our interview process, congratulations you have qualified ..." at the bottom of the letter it said 'are going to America.'

"Linda you passed!" the lady yelled to Mom before she could make her way upstairs.

Mom came racing back downstairs and almost fell head first into the woman. We all grabbed each other and started rejoicing and laughing. Afterward, Mom told us to stop because other people did not make it. She wanted to be respectful of them. The following week we were instructed to pack our stuff. We watched as those who were staying behind enviously went about their business; others spoke badly about us. Still, others cried with us and bid us farewell. We were picked up on the bus, brought to the airport and went through customs. When we got there, we were given a suitcase with winter coats. We sat under a tent with a bunch of other people until we were called. We were given our package and on the package it said which country we were going to and which state. Ours read United States of America Concord, NH. Mom was afraid to get on the plane, but she somehow mustered enough courage to get on.

We were seated by a beautiful flight attendant, a blonde haired blue eyed woman. I sat on the window seat. The waiting felt like forever. As the plane started to take off, I watched my mother as she started to shed tears. I felt my heart break again. My belly sank, I wanted to close my eyes to escape the feeling because it was hard to think. I looked out of the window once more; I saw as the illuminated city of Abidjan slowly become smaller and smaller until it disappeared. Behind each seat of the plane was a screen and each screen played a movie. The flight attendant went up and down with a tray of different types of food. Each time she would go by she would smile at me and wave. The plane ride felt like forever.

"Mom I need to pee," I said to Mom.

Mom got the flight attendants attention, "my son needs to pee," said Mom in her strong Liberian accent.

"Yes of course, follow me," said the flight attendant.

I followed the flight attendant to the back of the plane; she knocked on the bathroom door. Another young gentleman had just finished using the facilities and walked out.

"Thank you," I said to her in French, and she smiled and walked away.

I went inside the bathroom when I closed the door it wouldn't lock. I figured there was something wrong with it. After trying to close it for so long, I nearly peed myself. Finally, I saw a switch on the back, so I turn the switch on, closed it, and it worked. After using the facility, I went back and sat with Mom. Sophie had just woken up, and she also needed to use the bathroom, so I took her to the back of the plane and showed her how to open and close the door. I was fascinated by the plane and all its parts; I didn't want to go to sleep. Later on, I got tired and fell into a deep slumber. When I woke up, it was daytime, but we were still in the air. A few hours later I heard people point out the window and say, "look at the statue."

I looked around to try to see what they were pointing at but I couldn't see it. Mom and Sophie saw it, and they pointed it out, but I just couldn't see it. All I saw was the magnificent views of the towering buildings and beautiful landscape. The plane slowly descended and landed on the runway. Everyone got off the plane. In the airport was a person holding a sign with our name on it. We followed that person and they brought us to get our luggage. Then we waited a little while and got another plane that brought us from the beautiful city of New York to Manchester, New Hampshire. At our arrival, there was a lady with blonde hair with bangs wearing a peacoat waiting for us.

She recognized us right away because we just didn't fit in like the others.

She approached us and asked Mom, "Hi are you Linda Tar … wo?"

"Yes I am," Mom said smiling back at her.

"My name is Natalie welcome to America. I work for Lutheran Services I will be your caseworker for the next few months until you settle in."

"Okay," Mom said while keeping a smile.

Natalie helped us with our luggage; she brought us to her car to put our stuff in the trunk. Sophie and I sat in the back passenger seats while Mom sat in the front seat. She advised us to put on our seatbelts on. After that, we got on the highway and not long afterward we reached our final destination.

"Alright we're here," Natalie said. She got us into the apartment and showed us how the doorbell worked, how the stove worked, how the shower worked and so forth. The apartment was a bedroom apartment with two beds Sophie and Mom shared the larger bed while I took the smaller one. We had a living room and attached to the living room was a balcony which Mom wouldn't let me go on, but I would sneak out to it once in awhile. Natalie gave us her number and then told us she would be back early in the morning. The fridge was filled with food of different sorts, but most of the food didn't taste good to us, so we just made tea and bread. The next morning Natalie came early just like she said. She rang the doorbell, but we were still sleeping. Then Mom heard it and jumped out of bed to go answer.

"Who is it?" Mom asked.

"It's Natalie!" she said excitedly.

That morning she took us to go shopping at Goodwill, we were able to get some clothes and some shoes as well as a toy. Not long afterward we were able to install a house phone. That way, Natalie could reach us without surprising us every time she came unexpectedly. Mom started a new job; she started working early shifts, and a van would pick her up every morning except on weekends. She would get back home at noontime and cook for us. Sophie and I would stay inside and entertain ourselves by playing board games and watching TV. Then all the fun went away when Natalie came over and told Mom that Sophie and I needed to be enrolled in school. The last thing that I wanted to do was go to school. That week we went to go visit Dame Elementary School. It was an early morning; the sun was not yet up, and there was dew on the ground. The school playground was filled with kids running around. We walked into the office and told the lady at the front desk that we were here to see the principal.

The first thing the lady asked was, "do you have an appointment?" Nathalie stood confident and confirmed the time she booked her appointment. The lady checked in her system and saw that her name was there. "Take a seat please, he's finishing up a meeting he will be right with you guys."

The teachers all stepped out of the meeting, some said hi and smiled at me while others continued. Then finally an older gentleman with a white beard came out after they had all left. He seemed glad to see us, and it looked like he was expecting us. He asked Sophie and I simple questions and asked us if we were excited to go to school which we both smiled and nodded our heads yes. He and Natalie talked afterward, we shook his hand and got back in the car to go back home. While heading back home, Natalie showed Mom a shortcut to get to the school. Sophie ended up going to the Immaculate Heart Preschool right next to the Catholic Church across from where we lived; her walk was much shorter. After dropping Sophie off, she would then dropped me off at Dame school.

On the first day of school, Mom walked Sophie to preschool across the street while Nathalie walked me to Dame, a few blocks down the road. When we got there, the first thing she told me to do was to go check out the playground. I realized that mostly all of the kids did not look like me. On top of that, they didn't dress like me. I automatically feel out of place after standing around in the playground and being stared at by a bunch of kids.

Natalie came and got me when the bell rang; she excitingly escorted me to my class and at our arrival she and the teacher exchanged greetings. She introduced me to Miss Moore and briefly told her my story. Miss Moore looked at me, and asked with a smile, "Is that true?" I shyly nodded my head up and down looking away to avoid eye contact with her deep blue eyes. Miss Moore then introduced me to the class and asked me if I had anything to share. I looked up and saw all eyes piercing through me; I didn't know what to do or say. Miss Moore saw that I couldn't talk in front of a class, so she dismissed the kids for "quiet time," when everyone goes and reads a book individually. During recess, I was instantly recognized as a new face on the playground. Some kids in my class approached me and asked me about Africa and what it was like. I told them my story, and in the end, they all seemed shocked and amazed, others didn't know what to make of it. I came to realize my story was unique in that not every 7 year old had to go through war. That was the least of my worries. I came across not such nice kids on the playground who would point at me, giggle and then run off. School slowly started to become a nightmare. I remember one time when I was swinging on the swing. A kid pointed at me and said, "Mom look, it's a black."

I looked around, and I saw nobody else. I figure it was me he was pointing at. The kid's mother snickered and told her kid to stop. Multiple times I had to run away from other kids trying to pick a fight or ended up in a fight.

In class, I had a hard time comprehending the stuff the teacher was teaching. My first teacher was my 2nd-grade teacher Miss Moore. She was a nice woman fit and tall with a bright smile. Outside of school she would come and visit my family. She took my sister Sophie and I out for breakfast and introduced us to pancakes for the first time. She saw that I was far behind, learning-wise, so she did all that she could to get me the right help that I needed. After our morning meetings in class instead of doing the assignments as the other kids, I would be taken out of class by a reading teacher for some English 101. The poor lady would spend countless amount of time trying to teach me how to read and spell. I could almost feel her pain as I would memorize a sentence and get it right the first time but completely forget the second time.

At lunchtime, I sat alone because none of the other kids invited me to sit with them. I remember sitting at the peanut table and having a peanut butter sandwich because I couldn't read "No Peanuts Allowed". The other kids got scared and left the peanut table. The whole time I thought it was me they were afraid of until one day the lunch lady told me that I couldn't eat peanut at that table because someone allergic could get seriously hurt. I didn't know what I was doing. The one thing I hated most was recess time because I was always picked on and bullied. I started hating going to school; I didn't know who to tell so I would try to figure ways not to go to school. I heard a term called hooky being used by one of my schoolmates. This is when you play sick, so you don't have to attend class. So I tried playing hooky with my Mom and it worked, but soon enough she started catching on to it.

The leaves were changing colors; a cold front had come in affecting the temperature that day. The school bell rang, and class was dismissed. I waited outside the school and watched as other parents came and picked up their kids. I wasn't sure if Mom or Nathalie was picking me up, I waited for about an hour. After I saw no one was coming to get me, I started to make my way back home crying and clenching my hands in my shirt. This was the first time I've ever felt the cold like this. When I got home, my Mom buzzed me in. When I came in she saw tears rolling down my eyes, she came over and asked, "What is it?"

I showed her my fingers, "I am hurt from the cold," I told her.

"Go and run it under the hot water,' she told me, "don't cry, God will provide. Let's pray about it."

Sophie, Mom and I got down on our knees, held hands, and prayed. Afterward, we ate and watched News 9 before going to sleep. The next morning Mom walked Sophie and I to school just like she usually did every morning. As she was making her way back home, a gentleman hollered at her. She looked to see who it was. The man was sitting on his porch wearing a pair of shades.

"Hey you?" he said again.

"Yes," Mom said bewildered.

"My son and your son are friends, they go to the same school," the gentleman explained.

"That's wonderful," Mom said.

"If there is anything we can help you with please let us know," he added.

My mother and I saw the opportunity and knew that perhaps that was the answer to the prayer, she didn't waste any time. She walked over to their yard and told the man our case, how we didn't have winter clothes and boots. The man helped Mom make a list of things that we needed.

"Alright thank you, Linda," he said shaking her hand, "when my wife comes home I'll share this with her."

A few days later he and his wife came to our house with a truck full of supplies. They made it right on time because that night was also the first snowstorm of the winter.

"This is for you and your kids," Mrs. Milligan said.

They brought us winter jackets, boots, gloves backpacks with school supplies, toys and more things. They also went above and beyond by giving us bikes so that Sophie and I could get to school on our own. It felt like a miracle and later on, Daniel Milligan, her son, and I became best friends. He was infatuated with gadgets and technology, so he taught me about different types of techs. His sister and Sophie were the same age, so they became good friends.

When we woke up the following morning, it felt like someone had turned the heat all the way down. I overheard Mom talking about snow on the ground on the phone. I got out of bed to go see what she was talking about. When I opened the porch curtains, I saw white piles of stuff everywhere on the ground. My classmates have told me about snow, but this was my first time seeing it. I wanted to go outside and play in the snow like the other kids, but my Mom didn't want me to.

As time went on, Natalie started coming to our house less and less. Other people in the African community started visiting us though there wasn't that many of them during that period.

A lady named Shane "Lambardi" Dubius, would pay Mom regular visits, she quickly became a friend of the family. On Sundays, she would come get Mom to go to church in Manchester Pastored by a man named Chris Ineu. Mom would get Sophie, and I ready each Sunday morning, and then we would all go together. Then one day unexpectedly I bumped into her in school.

"Ms. Lambardi," I said excitingly.

She looked back and tried to figure out who I was. As she got closer, she realized it was me. Out of school, Ms. Lambardi spent a lot of time with Sophie and me. She would take us to her family's house for dinner. On a special occasion, she would take us out to the movies. Sometimes when I misbehaved, Mrs. Lombardi would correct me and tell me that's not the way I should be acting.

When Christmas was approaching, she asked us if we had a Christmas tree. My family didn't know what a Christmas tree was, but when I went over Dan Milligan's house, their family had a tree sitting in the middle of the room. My family thought it was silly, but it was an American tradition that we weren't familiar with. We decided that we were going to try to get a tree. Ms. Lombardi promised to get us a tree.

Yet she didn't have the means to do it so she asked someone else if they could get us a tree. On Christmas Eve, we got a tree, it was one of those manufactured trees, but it was still a tree. We were able to celebrate Christmas just like everybody else that year. A few months later, I was enrolled in the Boys and Girls Club. The staff liked me, and they were attentive to everything that was going on. I learned how to make friends and not make enemies by going to the Boys and Girls Club and sometimes it was hard. During our free time I played basketball and quickly began falling in love with the game. As time went by Ms. Lombardi moved away just like Natalie, but new people came. School was over and summer was at the door.

Summer came with its unbearable heat, summer in Africa was nothing compared to summer in NH. There was one holiday no one told us about, but we were soon going to find out. That night was just like the other ones until we started hearing loud explosions. We didn't know what was going on, to us it sounded like machine guns and heavy artilleries. We tried to find a place to hide. We left everything we had and made a run to one of Mom's friend's house. When we got there, everyone was sitting calmly and watching TV.

"What are you guys doing here at this time?" Mom's friend questioned.

"We heard guns, we needed a safe place to go," Mom responded concerned.

They started laughing, "That's not guns, that's the fireworks. They're celebrating the Fourth of July the American Independence Day," Mom's friend said trying to catch his breath.

We sat down with them and talked. We joked about the situation; I felt relieved, I was glad we didn't have to run away again. 3rd grade came around fast that year, I went to Broken Ground Elementary School for half of 3rd grade. Then Mom, Sophie and I moved downtown Jennings Drive. Sophie was in her first grade, so she and I would walk to Walker School together following the footprints on the ground. After school Sophie and I would take the bus together to the Greater Central Boys and

Girls Club downtown known as the big Boys and Girls Club.

During a group meeting, I heard that the Boys and Girls Club was going to be holding tryouts for the upcoming season for basketball. I was excited about the whole situation; it sounded like a great opportunity to showcase what I could do. I went over to Bob who was one of the staff and told him that I wanted to play basketball.

"Well if you want to play basketball," Bob said, "you're going to need basketball shorts and basketball shoes."

I knew I didn't have any of those things and Mom couldn't afford to get me those. I struggled with whether or not I should tell him and as he started walking off I ran behind him. I secretly pulled him off to the side and told him my condition. He looked at me contemplating what he should do next; then he told me to go play. In the meantime, he went off and talked to the other staffs and called me over afterward. Bob and another staff named Dusty and I got into one of the Boys and Girls Club minivan. We drove to Dick's Sporting Goods, and they got me some shorts and basketball shoes. I felt overwhelmed and happy that they would do that for me. Bob told me to show up on a certain day to try out to see if I can make the team.

On that day, I rode my bike down the snowy hill that Sophie and I walked every day after we left the Boys and Girls Club. I had my basketball shorts on and my new shoes in my bag. When I got to the Boys and Girls Club, there was a bunch of new faces, a bunch of other kids who were also trying out. Their parents sat in the bleachers and watched them. I put on my shoes, went on the court and started shooting the ball with the other kids. The coaches blew the whistle and called us over and discussed why we were there. They explained that not everybody was going to make the team and that would be determined by how hard we work. We did some conditioning and then we did some drills and scrimmaged a little bit. After the second tryouts as I was heading out, I came across a man by the name of Donald Jewell. He was a tall guy, scuffed clean shave and had a very inviting smile. Don was impressed by the way I played and wanted to congratulate me, "what's your name?" He asked.

"My name is Martin Toe," I said in a thick accent.

"Mahin what?" he asked trying to figure out my last name.

After repeating it the fourth time, I pointed at my toes which were poking out of my beaten up shoes. One of Don's friend offered to give me a ride back home because of the snow storm that was falling that night. During the basketball season, Don's son Garrett and I became really good friends. After 3rd grade, I moved down South Street where Vinnie Pizza is located. When 4th grade came around, I started going to Conant Elementary school. That year Garrett and I had the same class together and became close friends. We played sports together and hung out with other teammates. Don became a coach and a friend to my family and to a bunch of other kids who played on the team.

Playing sports gave me a platform and people started to recognize me. People I didn't know would come up to me and tell me that they had seen my name in the newspaper. They would congratulate me on my performance. It was weird, but I started getting used to it.

When 5th grade came around, it was an exciting time for because I had one more year until Junior High and plus I had the coolest 5th-grade teacher Mr. Gajowski also known as "Mr. G." He was a well-built, athletic fellow with lots of gray hair and an awesome smile. Mr. G's classes weren't like all the other classes; He had MacBook laptop he also incorporated as part of our learning. He showed us how to make power points, edit and make movies on a MacBook and also how to burn it to a CD. Just like Miss Moore, Mr. G saw that I was struggling to grasp the concepts that we were being taught in class, but he admired that I asked for help even when the occasion was embarrassing. Throughout my elementary and most of my middle school years, I needed extra help. Mr. G went out of his way to make sure that I got the extra help without having me be left out of what was being taught. As time went on Mr. G and I started building trust and soon enough I was able to have deep, meaningful conversations about home life and about where I came from. It made me respect him as a person because I knew he cared genuinely about me as a person.

I remember one day before going to school; I went to the Rite-aid on my way to class to buy a drink. While I was getting the drink, I saw an employee spying on me. I walked over a couple of aisles down to the candy area to see if she would follow me. Then out of nowhere, I saw her poke her head around a shelf and then walk by as if she minded her own business. While walking out of the candy aisle to go pay for my drink, there was another kid who entered the store at the same time I did. I saw another kid about a year or two older than me grabbing candy and putting it in his pocket. I walked to the counter and paid for my drink; I watched as the kid walked out of the store without paying for his candy. When I went to school, I told Mr. G about the incident and why she wasn't suspecting the other guy of stealing. We talked about stereotypes and other issues that were connected to it. That year I came to understand that not everyone thought so fondly of me. People had their own perception of who I was. After 5th grade, I went over to Rundlett Middle school where I began to shine as an athlete and was respected by my peers and teachers for my musical talent and people skill. Each morning I would walk across the street to talk to Mr. G, he was always glad to see me. He and I would talk about my progress and I would listen to his advice on school social groups. He and I still keep in touch to this day.

There are some things that I have learned through my journey: I understand through my father's actions that forgiveness is a fresh start to building relationships. I understand through my sister Sophie that giving up on something you love is not acceptable. If you look past the trials and hardships, you can see blessings and joy.

Chapter 16

During my first few years in America until up to now, Mom's friends would always lecture Sophie and I before leaving the house. Their message would always sound the same. Make sure you stay in school and learn something that will build up your future so that one day you can help your mom, and make your country better.

Looking back then I can see the wisdom in what my Mom's friends were saying. They wanted me to become someone of value and not a burden and a liability to my family and society. They wanted me to get an education in hopes of changing the life of my family and creating opportunities for those presently here and those back home where I came from. That is the main reason and purpose for why I have written this book.

The Book of Proverbs states that "without a vision the people perish."

A lot of the people who came from foreign countries and even those who lived here their whole life have either forgotten or lived life with no purpose. You've probably heard the expression "what a waste of life" being thrown around. They take living in America for granted. Water which is a rare commodity is taken for granted. In some countries, you're lucky if you can drink clean water but here in America water flows freely for anyone who's thirsty. Some people complain about their shoes wearing out or their brand of shoes not being up to date while somewhere in America there's someone who doesn't have a foot to put shoes on. I have been here for thirteen years, and I haven't taken anything for granted.

It's important that we understand the reason why we are in America. What are your hopes and aspirations that you are trying to accomplish in America? My Mom's friends were right, the people who don't know their purpose in America will, unfortunately, waste their lives in America. I've seen it time and time again with new people from Africa, Nepal, Asia, Europe, etc. they come to America with a fresh slate, then they start being influenced by the pop culture. Soon they are dressing, talking and acting a certain way. Before you know it, it's too late- they make one false move, and they're in the wrong place at the wrong time. Their private affairs now become a public display, and their character and reputation are stained. Don't be that guy, don't get sucked into the pop culture or the stuff you see on TV or on the Internet. Be wise. Try to learn from those who've earned their respect, those respected and spoken well of so that you can avoid many troubles and heartaches. It's hard to succeed on your own. You need a mentor to guide you, someone, who has been through the system. Without mentorship, it is hard to succeed.

In the previous chapter, I talked about my Rite-Aid incident where I was being followed and watched by an employee. To make sure I wasn't stealing while two aisles down. Another kid who I didn't mention was a white kid also in the store at the same time. While I was buying a drink, he was busy stuffing his pockets with bags of sweets. Yet, I was the only one being monitored.

I understand that there are three main ways you can choose to filter the way you view people. You can either see people from the perspective base filter, the principle base filter, or the passive base filter. Let me expound on these three types of filters.

A perspective base filter is when you look at people from the opinion that you formulate about a person from looking at their outside appearance. The way that something looks like or the way you conceive it.

The employee working at the store was operating out of the perspective base filter. She saw a black kid probably not wearing preppy clothes and her perception was he must not have money. While a few aisles down is another kid dressed no different, smuggling candy but in their perspective, he looks innocent. As we can see perception is very deceptive in that it doesn't solidify your thoughts as being factual.

The second view is the principle base filter. Instead of making judgments about people from just your perception, this filter looks at people from a moral value standpoint. For example, instead of thinking this kid is on food stamp because he has hot lunch or this kid does drugs because he has dreads. Instead, your first action is to step back and see that person is part of society. That person is not a beggar but is valuable to society. The principle base filter is more concerned with learning about the person. Getting to know the person before formulating a judgment about who they think that person is. The principle base filter seek to understand people out of compassion.

The third filter is the passive base filter. This filter occurs when a person desires to want to know about someone or something, yet, doesn't take action to go and learn about that person or thing. Instead, they leave it for time to be the judge; as some would say, to let fate decide. People that operate out of the passive base filter usually miss out on awesome opportunities. To get to learn and be a part of something beautiful.

My challenge to you is to see people with principle base filter, not perception base filter. When you see a group of young kids riding their bikes or a stranger dressed in traditional clothing walking down the street, don't just see them and let your mind formulate a perception of who you think they are. Go and learn who they are, you might be surprised at what you can learn about your own life.

Concord High School Principal Gene Connolly exemplified this paradigm of what it's like to operate through the principle base filter. In his address to the 2015 Fall season Athletes, Gene takes an unusual approach, which he writes about in his speech. The following excerpt is quoted from the printed copy of the speech given to me by Gene's son Jim:

Good afternoon. I want to begin by sharing how

honored I am to be invited to speak to this wonderful collection of student athletes. I was also surprised that I was invited because I have lost my ability to speak.

I am going to qualify that. I have lost the use of my vocal chords but because of modern technology I have a machine that allows me to speak. While the voice is computer generated the words are all mine. However, all of you are missing my Boston accent; my new computer generated voice is called Tom. Tom is from somewhere outside of New England. I'm not sure where but I think he is from out in the mid west somewhere.

This afternoon I have decided not to give a speech about all the wonderful things you learn from competing in athletics. Instead, I am going to share observations that I have made since being diagnosed with a terminal disease eighteen months ago.

Pay Attention. I recently read an article about the danger of daydreaming. The author of the study was reporting that daydreamers are less happy with their lives than people who live in the Moment. We hear that term a lot. How it is important to live in the moment.

In all honesty, I am probably the last person who should give this advice. Truth is I did not appreciate this message until after I was diagnosed. For almost sixty years I have been guilty of always looking ahead and while that sentiment might have helped with my career. It didn't help me to appreciate all the wonderful moments in life. Now, I find myself living in the moment more than ever before and enjoying more.

Be Excellent. I remember like it was yesterday when

I got my first position as a school administrator. It was at Londonderry Middle School. The Principal was Nancy Meyers who within five minutes of me entering the building on that first day had me sit down and then told me to never say "Good enough." Because I was now working in Londonderry and people who were fortunate enough to work in Londonderry knew anything worth doing is done right and never good enough. I remind myself of that advice everyday.

Another quote that I find useful especially when I am tired and want to quit and be something less than excellent is the famous Vince Lombardi "Fatigue makes cowards of us all." Try that one out when it is late, you're tired, and you have homework due the next day.

Say Hello to Everyone You See. I am a proud graduate of Springfield College. While I learned many important lessons, there is one that I use everyday: to greet everyone. On the campus at Springfield it was expected that you acknowledge everyone all of the time. That was a real rule on campus.

For years I had stood, now I sit and greet students and staff as they enter the building. It has become a tradition at the school. I like it because the simple, effortless task of saying hello usually brings a smile to the receiver's face.

Have Courage. Three years ago our senior class invited CHS alumna and Olympic Gold Medalist Tara Mounsey to speak at their graduation. One of her messages that day was for the graduates to have courage. During the last eighteen months, I have found myself thinking about her message often. Courage can take many forms. People who are courageous may be frightened and afraid but they summon the strength to do the right thing.

Think Before You Speak. Now that I have to type my words into a program I am forever behind in conversations. Many times I will be typing frantically to say something brilliant and by the time I finish typing and I look at my message and I erase it because it really wasn't that insightful or important.

Losing my ability to speak has forced me to be a better listener. It is not that I was a poor listener before but I have become an excellent listener. Now I have more than a person's words. I have a greater sensitivity to a person's tone, the nonverbal message that is every bit as important as the words. This will not be of use for you this afternoon listening to me. As I told you before my voice is named Tom and he is from the mid west and is free of emotion.

Embrace Gratitude. Expressing thanks for all you have is a lost emotion in our society. If you are ever in the neighborhood come by and visit Concord High School. Over fifteen percent of our students were not born in this country. Most spent significant time in refugee camps and after years of waiting to be vetted they were sent to Concord, New Hampshire for resettlement. Unlike other communities the city of Concord celebrates their arrival. They enrich us with their culture while we share ours. And of all the lessons they share with us the most important is that we need to be grateful for all that we have. Because if you ask them about their journey, they will tell you there are no bad days living in the United States.

Don't be afraid tell someone that you love them.

When I was in high school and college, it was the height of uncoolness to tell someone that you love them. And I followed the rules. Well, I am going to give you permission this afternoon to break the rule. The new rule is if you love someone you have to tell them.

Tell the truth. Randy Pausch was a professor at Carnegie Mellon. When his doctors told him he had cancer and that it was terminal, he gave an interview. The interviewer asked him if he had only three words that he could pass on what would he say, Pausch replied "Tell the Truth" the reporter not impressed with the answer ask him if he had another three words what would he say. Pausch replied "All the Time."

Family Comes First. I realize that you have heard this bit of advice before. I want to give you first-hand testimony how true it is. I am one of seven children and my wife one of nine. The amount of love bestowed on me from Patty's and my siblings has been overwhelming - the notes, hugs and kisses remind me how lucky I am to be a part of such an incredible family.

Since getting sick, my daughter and her husband Ryan moved back to Concord and my son moved back home. They have been part of an inner circle of folks who take care of my daily needs. And let me share with you I have become a lot of work.

Lastly let me tell you about my wife Patty, who teaches and coaches in Hopkinton. In fact one of her athletes Ireland Tawney is in attendance this afternoon. Patty and I will be celebrating our thirty-fifth wedding anniversary later this month. Patty has always been the center of our family. We have raised two talented kids who are both educators and coaches. Our son Jimmy teaches English at Winnacunnet High School and our daughter Allie teaches fourth-grade in Concord. Soon after being diagnosed I realized that Patty had it worst then I do. When we were married thirty-five years ago, it wasn't supposed to end like this. We had started talking about retiring to Cape Cod and getting old together living by the ocean. The reality is that plan is up in the air.

Life is not for the faint of heart it can be cruel and unfair. Living a fulfilling life can be challenging. Our job is to live our lives with purpose. No one can do it alone. You need the love and support of your family to give you the strength to deal with life's challenges.

That is the end of my list. Let's review. ***Pay Attention, Be Excellent, Say Hello to Everyone You See, Have Courage, Think Before You Speak, Embrace Gratitude, Don't Be Afraid to Tell Someone That You Love Them, Tell The Truth, and Family Comes First.***

Thank you for letting Tom speak for me.

I hope this book gets into the right hands, people who are willing to sit down and hear your story. I hope this book gets into the hands of a young refugee or someone with a good heart who cares about people. I hope a kid curious with good ambition picks up this book. Someone who is eager to make a difference his life and the life of his family and in the life of his people. I hope the world hears your story and becomes inspired. You are valuable.